The INTERNMENT of JAPANESE AMERICANS

Charlotte Taylor and Deborah Kent

Enslow Publishing
101 W. 23rd Street
Suite 240
New York, NY 10011
USA

Published in 2016 by Enslow Publishing, LLC
101 W. 23rd Street, Suite 240, New York, NY 10011

Cataloging-in-Publication Data
Taylor, Charlotte.
The internment of Japanese Americans / by Charlotte Taylor and Deborah Kent.
p. cm. — (Our shared history)
Includes bibliographical references and index.
ISBN 978-0-7660-7008-0 (library binding)
1. World War, 1939-1945 — Japanese Americans. 2. World War, 1939-1945 — Evacuation of civilians — United States. 3. Japanese Americans — Evacuation and relocation, 1942-1945. I. Taylor, Charlotte. II. Kent, Deborah. III. Title.
D769.8.A6 T39 2016
940.53'1773—d23

Printed in the United States of America

CONTENTS

Japanese Americans await internment in 1942.

The Journey Begins

He had become a man without a country. The land of his birth was at war with America . . . He was suddenly a man without rights who looked exactly like the enemy.

—From *Farewell to Manzanar*[1]

Mary Matsuda will never forget the day her world changed forever. It was December 7, 1941, and she was sixteen years old. She and her older brother, Yoneichi, walked home from church as they always did. It felt like a normal day. But that all changed as soon as they walked into their house. One look at their parents' distraught faces and they knew something was very wrong. Their father broke the news: The Japanese had bombed the US Naval Fleet at Pearl Harbor.

Mary Matsuda's parents were both born in Japan. They had immigrated to the United States as adults. In the new land, they were eager to build a better life for themselves and their children. They had lived in the

United States for many years, but they were still citizens of Japan. Under existing laws, Asian immigrants could never become US citizens. The situation was different for Mary and Yoneichi, of course. Born in the state of Washington, they were both automatically American citizens regardless of their ethnicity.

In the days after the bombing of Pearl Harbor in Hawaii, the United States went to war with Japan and Germany. The Matsuda family lived with mounting uncertainties. Mary had always felt safe on her family's strawberry farm. Now the world around her grew strange and threatening. Would Japanese planes drop bombs on West Coast targets? Would white Americans turn on their Japanese-American neighbors? Mary heard rumors that all Japanese Americans would have to be sent away from their West Coast homes. Would she and Yoneichi be sent away, despite the fact that they were US citizens?

Rumor became reality on February 19, 1942. On that day, President Franklin Delano Roosevelt signed Executive Order 9066. The presidential order gave the military the right to move "any and all persons" from parts of Washington, Oregon, California, and Arizona. It was understood that most of those to be moved would be Japanese Americans.

The Matsudas feared that they would have to leave their home. They would have to give up the farm, which they had developed through years of work. They had no idea where they might be sent. They did not know how they might be treated or how long they

Pearl Harbor: Missed Signs

A major reason for the devastation of the attack on Pearl Harbor was the element of surprise. But months before the bombings, the United States began receiving warnings that the Japanese might be planning an attack in the Pacific. Officials in the US War Department, however, dismissed these reports. Japan was too busy fighting in other areas of the world, the officials thought, and did not have the means to mount a successful attack on Hawaii at that point.

In November 1941, as tensions with Japan increased, US military heads sent messages to forces in the Pacific islands to prepare for war. Unfortunately, the commanders in Hawaii did little in way of preparation.

On the morning of December 7, 1941, more warnings were received and ignored. A group of planes spotted by radar as well as a suspicious submarine near the entrance to the harbor were both reported and dismissed. In addition, several hours before the attack, officials in Washington intercepted a message that threatened an imminent Japanese offensive. The warning was forwarded to Hawaii by telegraph and was not received until two hours after the bombings.[2]

The Japanese attacked the naval base at Pearl Harbor, Hawaii, on December 7, 1941.

might have to stay away. Living from day to day, they awaited further news.

One evening, a Japanese-American friend called with a frightening story. Agents from the Federal Bureau of Investigation (FBI) were inspecting the homes of Japanese-American families. Any evidence of ties with Japan was considered suspect. Some leaders of Japanese-American associations had been taken into custody. Mary Matsuda's father had served as secretary of their local Japanese-American Association. The association was a group that sponsored Japanese language classes and cultural events. Would the FBI take Mary's father to prison for his involvement with this group?

To prepare for the FBI inspectors, Mary's parents decided they must destroy all traces of their connection with Japan. On an evening in late February, they built a fire in the oil stove in their farmhouse living room. They gathered their Japanese books and phonograph records. They got out their photographs of relatives in Japan. They even brought out the beautiful Japanese dolls they always displayed on traditional holidays.

Sixty years later, Mary recalled the heartbreak of that long-ago evening:

> We stood in front of the table looking at all of our cultural treasures. . . . One by one [my father and mother] looked over each [phonograph] record and took turns breaking them, silently feeding their beloved music into the stove until every record was destroyed. . . . Our photographs of relatives in Japan came next. Together Mama-san and Papa-san looked at each picture with tired eyes, and talked about each person. Then they tossed the family photos into the burning stove, one by one.[3]

At last it was time for Mary's favorite Japanese doll to be burned. "Slowly I walked to the front of the stove, gave my doll one final squeeze, then flung her into the inferno that seared my heart like some fierce dragon destroying all that I loved," Mary remembered. "With tears streaming down my face, I turned away but I could still feel the heat and hear the roar of the flames as they consumed her delicate body in a matter of seconds."[4]

When the inspectors appeared a few days later, they found nothing suspicious at the Matsuda farmhouse. The only thing they took away was a .22 rifle that Yoneichi used to scare crows away from the strawberry fields. Nevertheless, Mary and her family knew that sooner or later they would be required to leave their home. Mary had lived in the United States all her life, and she had always considered herself a loyal American.

When she looked at her reflection in the mirror, however, she began to see herself as her Caucasian neighbors must see her:

> My hair was still coarse, straight, and black. My skin was yellow, and my bespectacled eyes were small and slanted. We tried to erase our Japanese history by destroying all those precious things, but we could not escape from the way we looked. Nothing could change that. And in the end, all that mattered to the United States government was what we looked like.[5]

On May 16, 1942, ushered by heavily armed soldiers, Mary, Yoneichi, and their parents boarded a train headed for an unknown destination. They were allowed to bring only what they could carry in two suitcases apiece. The train was crowded and dirty. Heavy shades covered the windows. The frightened passengers could not see where they were being taken. After a three-day journey, soldiers with rifles ordered the Matsudas and the other passengers off the train. Armored trucks carried them to the Pinedale Assembly Center. The center was a hastily constructed camp in the desert outside Fresno, California. It was

In 1942 these posters directed Japanese Americans in the San Francisco area to evacuate and assemble to be sent to the internment camps.

surrounded by steel fences topped with barbed wire. Searchlights swept the camp day and night. Soldiers with machine guns stood guard in watchtowers along the fence.

Mary Matsuda had never been accused of committing a crime. She had never stood trial nor was she given a chance to defend herself. Yet she, like thousands of other US citizens of Japanese ancestry, was held prisoner by the government of her own country.

The Camps: Choosing the Right Words

The US government called the camps "relocation centers." The terms "internment camp" and "internment center" have generally been used by camp survivors. On at least two occasions, President Roosevelt referred to the centers as "concentration camps." When most people think of concentration camps, they think of Auschwitz and other death camps created by Adolf Hitler in Europe.

Unidentified children look beyond the barbed wire at the Manzanar internment camp in California.

In Hitler's camps, millions of people died of starvation and over-work or were deliberately murdered. Certainly this was not the case in the United States. In some ways, however, the US camps resembled those in Europe. In both situations, people were imprisoned based on their racial or ethnic background. Japanese Americans were held in the United States and Jews and Gypsies were imprisoned in Europe. In both cases, prisoners were held without charges or trial. Therefore, some historians and camp survivors feel that the term "concentration camps" applies to the US centers.

In the first panic-stricken months of World War II, many white Americans believed that the Japanese Americans who lived along the West Coast posed a threat to national security.[6] They feared that people of Japanese ancestry had strong ties to Japan and would be disloyal to the United States. Japanese Americans might be spies, sending vital information by radio back to Tokyo. They might plan acts of sabotage, dynamiting factories or military bases. In the wake of the attack on Pearl Harbor, Roosevelt's order for the removal of Japanese Americans and Japanese-born aliens sounded like a wise precaution.

Executive Order 9066 sent some one hundred ten thousand men, women, and children of Japanese origin to internment centers. About two thirds of them were American citizens. Tens of thousands of these internees were held for the next three years, until the war was finally over. In many cases, families lost their homes, their businesses, and their life savings. Worse still, the internees endured the pain and humiliation of being tated as untrustworthy and undesirable members of American society.

The Japanese attack on Pearl Harbor triggered deep-seated fears and resentments toward Japanese immigrants and their children. To understand the complex factors that led to the Japanese-American internment of World War II, it is first necessary to examine the history of Japanese settlement along the West Coast of the United States.

Settling in America

Around 1895 a young Japanese man, after hearing of the many opportunities available in the United States, decided to head to America to seek his fortune. So at the age of seventeen, he made the trip across the Pacific Ocean from Japan to Oregon. Once he arrived, he planned to study and get a job. He had no doubt that, with some hard work and a quality education, he would soon be a success.

That young man quickly learned a hard lesson. Only the lowliest jobs were open to Japanese newcomers. Soon he found himself peeling potatoes and washing dishes at a Portland boardinghouse. His dreams of riches began to fade.

At first, the hard work and degrading treatment overwhelmed him. In his labored English, he wrote: "I thought I shall never be able to proceed the work. I felt as if I am pressed down on my shoulder with loaded tons of weight."[1] Nevertheless, he believed in himself and he was determined to succeed. When his employer treated him cruelly, he reminded himself, "I have a soul within me. My vital energy in self-denying struggle could not be impaired by your despise."[2]

The Japanese Arrive

The young man had come to the United States with the first group of Japanese immigrants. That first group began to arrive in 1867. Most of these early arrivals were young men from prosperous, educated families. The Japanese government hoped they would serve as ambassadors. They would show the heights of Japanese culture to the people of the United States. The immigrants hoped to attend American universities, paying their way by taking whatever work they could find. Because they attended classes, these young men were known as schoolboys. According to census figures, 6,395 of these schoolboys entered the United States between 1867 and 1902.[3] Many of these students returned to Japan. With them they carried exciting new knowledge of the world beyond their homeland.

In 1884, the Japanese government began to allow men of the landless working class to emigrate to Hawaii. Their labor was needed on the sugar plantations of the islands. The Japanese were willing to work hard for low wages. The sugar growers were delighted to take advantage of the new cheap labor supply.

After working in Hawaii, many Japanese immigrants moved to the Pacific Coast of the United States. They were lured to the mainland by the promise of better-paying jobs. In the United States, they worked

Many Japanese moved to Hawaii and the West Coast of the United States in the late 1800s.

in the railroad, timber, fishing, and farming industries. Like the schoolboys, most of these immigrants were young, single men. Unlike the students, however, they had little wish to return to Japan. Japanese society had a rigid class structure. If a man was born a landless peasant, he would probably be a peasant all his life. The United States offered the possibility of change. With hard work, a man could save money and buy land or start a business. The immigrants planned to stay in the United States, building new and better lives.

The beginning of the twentieth century was a time of vast immigration to the United States. In 1900 some four hundred thousand immigrants flocked to America's shores. The vast majority crossed the

Atlantic and landed at Ellis Island in New York. Most of them came from eastern and southern Europe. Only a tiny fraction of the new arrivals were immigrants from Japan. The Japanese did not enter the country at Ellis Island. They crossed the Pacific and landed at ports on the West Coast. The 1900 census showed that 24,788 Japanese immigrants were living in the United States.[4] Most of them had settled along the Pacific Coast, in Washington, Oregon, and California.

Life for the immigrants was filled with hardships. Wages were low, and workdays were long. Many jobs were dangerous. In Oregon and Washington, Japanese immigrants worked to clear land for farming. Timber companies had harvested the trees that grew on the land. They left behind thousands of ragged, deep-rooted stumps. The stumps had to be removed before farmers could plant their crops. "A lot of people were using dynamite," one Japanese immigrant remembered many years later. ". . . Then you'd dig the roots out and cut them with the ax. Then you get the horse to pull. Boy, that's a lot of hard work!"[5]

In many ways, hard work brought success to the immigrants from Japan. They saved money and leased land or started businesses. They sent their children to school, hoping they could become teachers, doctors, or engineers. Nevertheless, they faced a climate that was sometimes hostile. Some Americans of European descent felt that the Japanese would always be outsiders. They argued that the Japanese could never assimilate, or fit in, to the American way of life.

The same complaints were leveled at immigrants from Italy, Russia, and other eastern and southern European countries. Some Americans felt that the European immigrants would ruin the United States. The newcomers were poor and uneducated, and they spoke an assortment of foreign languages. The Europeans, however, came from a culture that was similar to that of the United States. Above all, they had white skins. They looked like most of the Americans around them. Within a generation or two, they adopted American ways and were fully accepted.

People from Japan could not blend in so easily. Their complexions and facial features marked them as different. Even their children, born in the United States, could always be spotted as Japanese.

Chinese Struggles

People from Japan were not the first Asians to reach the United States. They were preceded by a group of immigrants from China. Chinese immigration began in 1849, and it played a major role in settling the West Coast.

In 1848 a rancher discovered gold in a riverbed in northern California. The news swept across the continent. Soon thousands of gold seekers headed to California from the eastern states. Rumors of fantastic wealth also flashed across the Pacific to faraway China. Eager young men set out from China to join the California gold rush. Few of these men found riches in the gold fields. White Americans often pushed them off their claims. However, the Chinese saw that

California offered other opportunities. Many became businessmen, serving the needs of the miners. They sold food and tools and opened laundries to wash the miners' dirty clothes.

More and more people poured into California from the east. By wagon or stagecoach the trip was long and dangerous. A railroad across the continent would be a safe, fast link between east and west. Thousands of Chinese workers were hired to build the western branch of the Transcontinental Railroad. By 1870, about one of every ten Californians was Chinese.[6]

When the railroad was completed in 1869, the Chinese began to compete for other jobs. Chinese workers were often hired first because they were willing to work for low wages. White Americans, quickly grew resentful. White workers held anti-Chinese rallies in San Francisco and other cities. They shouted that the United States was a white man's country where the Chinese would never be welcome. One supposed expert, a man named Dr. S. Wells Williams, described the Chinese in a widely read book. "There is nothing which tries one so much . . . as their disregard of truth," he wrote; ". . . The patience is exhausted when in daily proximity and friction with this ancestor of sins."[7]

In 1871 a mob swept into the Chinese section of Los Angeles. Before order was restored, twenty Chinese men had been shot or hanged. The US government bowed to the rising anti-Chinese pressure. The Chinese Exclusion Act of 1882 ended immigration from China to the United States.

Employers on the West Coast soon missed the steady supply of new Chinese workers. Farmers wanted low-paid laborers to harvest their crops. City dwellers wanted inexpensive cooks, gardeners, and housekeepers. Workers from Japan began to meet the growing need. They, too, were willing to accept low wages in return for long days of exhausting toil.

A Hostile Environment

"The Japs Must Go!" blared a headline in White River, Washington, in 1894. White workers in the region had come to resent the Japanese. Caucasian farmworkers accused the Japanese of working for "starvation wages."[8] They claimed that cheap Japanese labor made it impossible for white Americans to earn a living. White farmworkers called on farmers to stop hiring Japanese laborers. Within a few months, most Japanese workers had been driven out of the White River area.

The turmoil in White River reflected the growing hostility toward immigrants from Japan. Like the Chinese, the Japanese were seen as a threat to American workers. Some whites even claimed that the Japanese were eroding the American way of life. They came from a culture that was not European. Some were Christians, but many followed other religions. In 1900 Mayor James Duval Phelan of San Francisco declared, "The Chinese and the Japanese are not bona fide citizens. They are not the stuff of which American citizens can be made."[9]

Under American law, Japanese immigrants could never become American citizens. The first generation

This 1924 photo shows a group of Japanese immigrants who settled in Oregon.

Japanese immigrants were known as *Issei*, a Japanese term. The children of the Issei who were born in the United States were citizens automatically. They had all the rights of anyone else born within the country's borders. The American-born children of Japanese parents were known as *Nisei*.

The first Japanese immigrants had been single men. In the early 1900s, Japanese men began to send for wives to join them in their adopted land. Often they arranged marriages through a go-between in their home village. Through the go-between, the prospective bride and groom exchanged letters and photographs. A "marriage by proxy" was conducted in Japan while the groom was in the United States. In such a marriage, the bride took part in a ceremony though the groom

The Long Road to Citizenship

According to the Immigration Act of 1790, only "free white persons" could become naturalized citizens of the United States. A naturalized citizen is an immigrant who lives in the country for a given length of time and meets certain requirements. Once naturalized, he or she has all the rights of a person born in the United States. Changes were made to the Immigration Act in 1870. These changes followed the Civil War and the end of slavery. For the first time, persons of African ancestry were allowed to become citizens. However, the changes did not affect Asians. Persons born in Asia could not become naturalized citizens until 1952.

was absent. The "picture bride," as she was called, then sailed to America. In a strange new country, she joined the husband she had never seen.

Life could be harsh for Japanese picture brides. In rural areas, they worked beside their husbands in the fields. In the towns and cities, they often served as maids or cooks for white families. At home, they

Japanese "picture brides" came to the United States to marry men that they had never met before.

were expected to prepare meals, mend clothes, keep the house clean, and care for their children. In a traditional Japanese family, the wife was expected to obey her husband.[10]

In 1905 Japan defeated Russia in the Russo-Japanese War. Japan was becoming a major military power. Its navy was one of the finest on earth. As Japan grew stronger, the Japanese government felt that its citizens should be respected by the United States. Japan paid close attention to the way America treated the Issei and Nisei. Any sign of discrimination was considered an insult to Japan itself.

A decision by the San Francisco School Board in 1906 sparked a crisis between the United States and Japan. The school board had already established separate schools for children of Chinese and Korean descent. Now the board voted to send Japanese students to these separate schools as well. Asian children would be kept entirely apart from Caucasian pupils. The Japanese government was outraged. It threatened to cut off trade with the United States and even hinted about going to war. Finally, President Theodore Roosevelt became involved. After more than a year of talks, he completed a pact with Japan. This pact was called the Gentleman's Agreement. Roosevelt promised to urge the city of San Francisco to teach Nisei children along with white children in the public schools. In return, Japan agreed to stop allowing Japanese workers to immigrate to America. However, the Issei could still send for wives, children, and parents living in Japan. Picture brides continued to enter the United States until 1921.[11]

The Gentleman's Agreement did little to quench anti-Japanese feeling. Hostility toward the Japanese Americans still smoldered on the West Coast. American workers continued to resent the Japanese who accepted low wages. At the same time, they watched with dismay as Japanese farmers turned stump-choked land into productive acreage. It did not seem right, they grumbled, for foreigners to thrive while their white neighbors struggled.

In 1913 California passed a law stating that "aliens ineligible for citizenship" could not own land in the state.[12] By 1922, similar "Alien Land Laws" had passed in Washington, Oregon, New Mexico, Idaho, and

According to the Gentleman's Agreement, Japanese-American children were allowed to attend the same schools as white students in San Francisco. Here, a Japanese American and a white boy sit at a lunch table in their school in 1942.

Montana. Issei could no longer buy land. However, land could still be purchased through their children who were American citizens. The Alien Land Laws were another painful reminder that the Japanese were unwelcome.

In 1917 the United States joined the vast conflict known as the World War I. The war ended eighteen months later, in November 1918. Thousands of American veterans came home and began looking for work. On the West Coast, some found themselves

This World War I veteran is on his way to a relocation center in the 1940s, like many other Japanese Americans at the time.

competing with the Japanese for scarce jobs. The employment situation triggered a fresh burst of anti-Japanese feeling.

In 1920, a writer named Lothrop Stoddard published a book called *The Rising Tide of Color Against White World-Supremacy.* Stoddard warned that Japanese and other Asian immigrants could undermine the "superior race-culture" of the United States. He urged the nation to end all immigration from Asia. Stoddard's open racism struck a chord with many Americans. His book became a best-seller.[13]

Pressure from anti-Asian groups finally led Congress to pass a new immigration law. In 1924,

President Calvin Coolidge signed a bill known as the Asian Exclusion Act. The law closed the doors of the United States to immigration from all Asian countries, including Japan.

A Haven for the Japanese

During the 1930s, Sue Kunitomi grew up in the Japanese section of Los Angeles. The neighborhood was known to everyone as Little Tokyo. "It was a tightly knit community in which life was always busy," she writes, "and cultural activities filled the evenings and weekends of those who longed for their homeland. For the young people growing up in Little Tokyo, there was a sense of strength and protection from a hostile world."[14]

Many white employers refused to hire Issei and Nisei. In Little Tokyo, however, the Japanese set up their own businesses. Japanese grocery stores sold fresh fish and fragrant Japanese vegetables. Japanese-run hotels provided a home for Issei bachelors. People in Little Tokyo took their clocks to the Japanese-owned clock-repair shop.

Many families in Little Tokyo worshipped at the neighborhood's Buddhist temple. Buddhism is a religion practiced widely in Asia. Chinese and Japanese immigrants brought Buddhism to the United States. Not all Issei and Nisei were Buddhists, however. Many belonged to Baptist, Methodist, or other Protestant churches.

Sue Kunitomi and her Nisei friends thought of themselves as both Japanese and American. They celebrated

Japanese holidays, such as Girls' Day and Boys' Day. Their parents sent them to Japanese language classes after school. Some Nisei children learned Japanese martial arts, such as judo and kendo. At the same time, the children of Little Tokyo enjoyed American games and holidays. They exchanged presents at Christmas, dyed eggs at Easter, and watched fireworks on the Fourth of July. Nearly everyone, young and old, loved baseball.

The Japanese Americans—Issei and Nisei together—were known as the Nikkei. Before World War II, strong Nikkei communities were centered around three cities on the West Coast. Los Angeles, San Francisco, and Seattle each had large Japanese neighborhoods. In addition, many Japanese people

Little Tokyo in Los Angeles was a haven for Japanese Americans in the 1930s.

Believers in Buddha

The Buddhist religion was founded in India about 500 BC. Its founder, known as the Buddha, taught that each person passes through many lives, deaths, and rebirths. Our deeds in one life help determine the next life we will live. After many lives, a person's soul may reach a state of peace called nirvana.

Today Buddhism has 300 million followers. Most Japanese Buddhists belong to the branches of Buddhism called Zen and Mahayana. Most Buddhist temples in the United States have become Americanized. They hold services on Sundays, run Sunday schools for children, and host picnics and other social activities.

lived and worked in rural areas. A community of Japanese fishermen lived at Terminal Island off the coast of southern California. Japanese families worked on farms around Puget Sound in Washington and in California's Central Valley.

As Sue Kunitomi explains, the Japanese communities provided a feeling of safety. In contrast, the world outside could be harsh and unwelcoming. Issei and Nisei were generally seen as unskilled workers. Even if they had advanced training, they were seldom allowed

This Japanese-American family worked on a farm in Los Angeles, California.

to enter professions, such as medicine, law, or college teaching. Many college graduates found themselves unable to find good jobs. They ended up waiting on tables or picking strawberries. One discouraged young man wrote: "The only place where we are wanted is in positions that no American would care to fill . . . house-servants, gardeners, vegetable peddlers, continually 'yes, ma'am'-ing."[15]

As he searched for meaningful work, this young Nisei man ran into a wall of racial prejudice. Because of his Japanese background, he was not fully accepted in white American society. Prejudice against the Japanese Americans had deep and stubborn roots. When Japan bombed Pearl Harbor in 1941, that prejudice burst into full bloom.

State of Fear

Upon hearing the news of the bombing of Pearl Harbor, Japanese immigrants around America were thrown into a state of uncertainty. What would happen now? What did this mean for their future in America?

Amy Uno was one such immigrant. Only twenty-one years old, Amy was a live-in housekeeper for a white family. Immediately after the bombing, Amy's employers acted as though she could not be trusted. "They told me . . . how I had better stay at home until the FBI could clear me of any suspicion," Amy said years later. "I said, 'Why should I be suspected of anything? I've lived in your home for many years now. . . . And I never poisoned you once, and I'm not about to do it now.'"[1]

When Amy arrived home, she discovered a team of FBI officers at the house. "They were tearing out the floorboards, taking bricks out of the fireplace, and looking through the attic," Amy recalled. ". . . They tore part of the siding out on the side of our house to see if we were hiding things in between the walls."[2] The FBI men did not find any hidden weapons or secret papers. Nevertheless, they took Amy's father away with them. For the next six years, he was held in a series of prison camps. No charges were ever brought against him. He was held as a "hard-core enemy alien" until September 1947, two years after the end of the war.[3]

In the frantic days after the Pearl Harbor attack, 2,192 Issei (nearly all of them men) were arrested.[4] This amounted to nearly one in ten Japanese-American male adults on the West Coast.[5] In their eagerness to find suspects, the FBI seized on the slightest hint of

The day after the attack on Pearl Harbor, FBI agents rounded up groups of Japanese for detainment on Ellis Island.

wrongdoing. In the home of Masuo Yasui, an Oregon businessman, agents found crude diagrams of the Panama Canal. Yasui explained that his children had drawn the diagrams for a homework assignment. The agents did not believe his story. They were certain that Yasui was plotting to blow up the Panama Canal. Yasui was held in prison for the next four years.[6]

Most of those arrested were leaders within their Japanese-American communities. They were teachers, business owners, Protestant ministers, and Buddhist priests. Many taught Japanese to Nisei children after regular school hours. The US government believed that these Japanese immigrants had strong ties to their homeland. Government officials feared that they might be spies. They also worried that the Issei might try to sabotage, or purposely damage, factories and military bases. The government chose to hold suspected Issei in prison camps where they could do no harm.

The arrests filled Issei and Nisei with dread. Who would be next, they asked one another. Was anyone truly safe?

Meanwhile, among white Americans, rumors leaped from mouth to mouth. People claimed that Japan was about to attack California. Some said that spy planes had been seen over San Francisco. Many insisted that their Japanese neighbors were secretly helping the enemy.

The FBI seemed to be finding evidence against the Japanese Americans every day. From the homes of West Coast Issei the FBI seized 199,000 rounds of ammunition, 1,652 sticks of dynamite, 1,458 radio

The bombing of Pearl Harbor produced strong anti-Japanese feelings across much of the United States. This propaganda poster was issued shortly after the attack.

receivers, 2,914 cameras, and 37 motion-picture cameras.[7] Surely, people argued, this proved that the Issei were sending pictures and radio signals to warships offshore. Perhaps they planned to dynamite key bridges and tunnels. In fact, however, the Issei had nearly all of this material for their personal use. Hobbyists enjoyed using cameras and short-wave radios. Farmers had guns and bullets handy for shooting crows and rabbits that damaged their crops. Sometimes they used dynamite to blast stumps out of their fields.

For many Americans, outrage over the Pearl Harbor attack mingled with deep-seated anti-Japanese feelings. Japanese Americans became a ready target for blame and fury. Some Issei and Nisei were fired from their jobs. On the playground, Nisei children were pelted with the words, "Dirty Jap!" A San Francisco man printed posters that read: "Jap Hunting License, Good for Duration of Hunting Season, Open Season Now. No Limit."[8] In the *Saturday Evening Post*, the head of the Growers and Shippers Association of Salinas, California, spewed forth his hatred: "If all the Japs were removed tomorrow we'd never miss them," he wrote. "The white farmers can take over and produce everything the Jap grows. We don't want them back when the war ends, either!"[9]

Many Chinese Americans were frightened by this swirling anti-Japanese sentiment. They knew that many white Americans thought Japanese and Chinese faces looked the same. Perhaps the Chinese would be attacked, mistaken for Japanese Americans. To protect

Spies Among Us

Not all of the Japanese on the West Coast were loyal to the United States. Shortly before the war broke out, the US military seized a series of some five thousand cablegrams. Known as the MAGIC Cables, the cablegrams were written in a difficult code. The US military broke the code and discovered that the cables were very important. The messages showed that Japanese agents in the United States were sending information to Tokyo. A network of spies was working from within the Japanese consulates in Seattle, Los Angeles, and other cities. The Japanese government planned to expand its spy network. In some of the cables, Japanese agents planned to seek help from the Issei and Nisei. However, the cables showed that officials in Japan feared that the Issei and Nisei were not trustworthy.

The MAGIC Cables gave the FBI vital information. FBI agents arrested the spies and derailed Japan's plans.

themselves some Chinese Americans wore buttons that read, "I Am Chinese."[10]

Though the FBI's prime suspects had been arrested, some officials called for further steps. They suggested that all people of Japanese background should be "evacuated" from their homes along the coast. The evacuation plan called for the Japanese to be moved inland. They should not be allowed to live near important ports and factories. They should not have the chance to signal to Japanese ships or planes. An editorial in a Seattle paper had an anti-Japanese opinion. "I am for the removal of every Japanese on the West Coast to a point deep in the interior," the author stated. "I don't mean a nice part of the interior, either. Herd 'em up, pack 'em off and give 'em the inside room of the badlands. Let 'em be pinched, hurt, hungry and dead up against it."[11]

One of the loudest voices in favor of relocation was that of General John L. DeWitt. DeWitt headed the Western Defense Command, which was responsible for protecting the nation's Pacific Coast. He was convinced that Issei and Nisei were working in league with the Japanese government. The best way to protect the American people, DeWitt believed, was to relocate all of the Japanese families on the West Coast. DeWitt expressed his beliefs about the Japanese Americans in a report to the War Department on February 14, 1942. "The Japanese race is an enemy race," he wrote. ". . . It, therefore, follows that along the vital Pacific Coast over 112,000 potential enemies, of Japanese extraction, are at large today."[12]

In Washington, DC, President Franklin Delano Roosevelt listened to his generals and advisers. He read stacks of letters sent by ordinary citizens. At last he made his fateful decision.

The President Reacts

While he was attending Harvard University, young Franklin Roosevelt met several students from Japan. In 1902 he had a long talk with one of these Japanese students, Otohiko Matsukata. Matsukata told Roosevelt that Japan had a secret plan to control East Asia and the western Pacific. The plan involved the buildup of the Japanese Navy. Japan would then conquer Manchuria, China, and the Philippines.

Roosevelt never forgot his talk with Matsukata. He watched with concern as Japan built up its naval power during the 1910s and 1920s. Then, in 1931, Japan invaded Manchuria. Step by step, Japan seemed to be following the plan Matsukata had described.[13]

By early 1941, tension was high between Japan and the United States. The two nations hovered on the brink of war. Months before the bombing of Pearl Harbor, Roosevelt sent intelligence agents to study the Japanese-American community. He wanted to know whether the Japanese Americans were loyal to the United States, or if they would support Japan in the event of war.

On November 7, Roosevelt received a report on the Japanese Americans. The leading investigator stated:

> The Issei or first generation is considerably weakened in
> their loyalty to Japan by the fact that they have chosen

President Roosevelt

President Franklin Delano Roosevelt was born into a wealthy family in New York State. Franklin Roosevelt's family expected that he, too, would have a brilliant career in politics. Roosevelt's political career seemed to be over when he contracted polio in 1921. The disease destroyed the muscles in his legs and left him unable to walk. Despite his disability, Roosevelt returned to politics. In 1932, he was elected the thirty-second president of the United States.

When Roosevelt became president, the nation was in the grip of a terrible economic depression. Millions of people were fired from their jobs. Roosevelt worked to make life better for struggling Americans.

From 1941 until his death in 1945, Roosevelt led the nation through World War II. His decisive leadership won him praise at home and abroad.

Roosevelt was elected to four terms in office. On February 27, 1951, the Twenty-second Amendment to the Constitution was ratified, limiting a president to only two four-year terms in office. However, even before that, no other US president had ever served as long as Franklin D. Roosevelt.

Franklin Delano Roosevelt

to make this their home and have brought up their children here. . . . The weakest from a Japanese standpoint are the Nisei. They are universally estimated from 90 to 98% loyal to the United States. . . . They are pathetically eager to show this loyalty.[14]

After Pearl Harbor, Hawaii, was attacked, this report did little to protect the Japanese Americans. The government took severe measures against them, referring to them as "enemy aliens." The FBI searched homes and arrested suspected spies. The US Navy beached Issei-owned fishing boats for fear they could be used to contact Japan's warships. The bank accounts of Issei were frozen. Each Issei household was allowed to withdraw only one hundred dollars per month until the end of the war. To make matters worse, many employers fired their Japanese-American workers. Japanese-American families faced grinding financial hardships.

The Japanese Americans were not the only targets of anger and suspicion. The United States was also at war with Mussolini's Italy and the Germany of Adolf Hitler. Like the Japanese, Italian and German nationals in the United States were listed as "enemy aliens." Their bank accounts were frozen. Many were arrested and held without trial on suspicion that they might be plotting against the United States. However, there was no loud public outcry against people of Italian or German origin. As a group, the Japanese looked very much different compared to most Americans.

The US government posted this sign on Terminal Island in California ordering all Japanese, German, and Italian immigrants to leave the area by midnight February 24, 1942.

Caucasian Americans often described them with the words *inscrutable*, *unknowable*, and *untrustworthy*. Even President Roosevelt expressed racial prejudice. In 1942, he told one of his advisers that the Japanese were "a treacherous people." In a private conversation, he repeated a Chinese folktale that claimed the Japanese had descended from a baboon.[15]

Most Japanese Americans wanted to show that they were loyal to the United States. The Japanese American Citizens League (JACL), a leading Japanese-American organization, sent a telegram to President Roosevelt days after Pearl Harbor. "In this solemn hour we pledge our full cooperation to you, Mr. President, and to our country," the telegram read. "There cannot be any question, there must be no doubt. We, in our hearts, know we are Americans—loyal to America. We must prove that to all of you."[16]

Meanwhile, General DeWitt called for immediate action to prevent disaster. He urged the creation of military zones along the West Coast. All enemy aliens—German, Italian, and especially Japanese— should be moved away from these special areas. Secretary of War Henry L. Stimson took up the cry. He argued for the mass removal of all Japanese from the West Coast. This removal would include US citizens as well as aliens.

The US Constitution guarantees American citizens the right to a fair trial. The Fifth Amendment to the Constitution states that no person may be "deprived of life, liberty or property, without due process of law." To remove Japanese Americans from their homes and confine them against their will seemed a clear violation of their rights under the Constitution. However, the president has the right to set constitutional laws aside in a time of national crisis. The Constitution itself grants this emergency power to the president. President Abraham Lincoln claimed this executive privilege during the crisis of the Civil War. Those who favored removal of the Japanese Americans argued that the nation was in a severe crisis once again. In this national emergency, the president could suspend the constitutional rights of the Japanese Americans.

As a wartime president, Roosevelt's first concern was the security of the American people. He paid close attention to his generals and to the secretary of war.

Soldiers stand guard as Japanese-American citizens board trains to their internment at the Santa Anita racetrack in California.

Roosevelt believed that they understood the realities of war, and he took their advice very seriously.

On February 19, 1942, Roosevelt issued Executive Order 9066. The order called for the creation of military zones along the West Coast. "Any and all" civilians could be removed from these areas, as the military saw fit. The order did not single out people of a particular race or nationality. Nevertheless, it was used for the removal of all Japanese Americans.

Many German and Italian citizens were also removed from the West Coast under Executive Order 9066. However, most of them were quickly given hearings and allowed to prove that they were not dangerous to the United States.[17] The Japanese Americans were treated very differently. Even the Nisei, who were American citizens, were taken from their homes and confined to relocation camps. Without charges or hearings, they were locked away behind barbed wire. Roosevelt's attorney general, Francis Biddle, wrote years later: "the decisions were not made on the logic of events or on the weight of evidence, but on the racial prejudice that seemed to be influencing everyone."[18]

Relocation

Executive Order 9066 sent waves of shock through the Japanese-American community. At first, most Japanese Americans thought that only Issei would be relocated. They assured themselves that Nisei, who were American citizens, would be allowed to remain in their homes. However, on March 2, 1942, the army

Hawaii Escapes Internment

In 1941 Hawaii was a territory of the United States. About one hundred fifty thousand people of Japanese origin lived in Hawaii. The Japanese made up about one third of Hawaii's total population. At first the US government hoped to intern all of the Hawaiian Japanese. However, the governor of Hawaii felt that mass internment would cause huge problems on the islands. Hawaii needed Japanese laborers to work on its sugar plantations and farms. Without the Japanese, the economy of the islands would collapse. Mass internment of Hawaiian Japanese never took place. Some Japanese Hawaiians were imprisoned on the islands. Only about eleven hundred were shipped to internment camps on the mainland.[19]

announced that all people of Japanese origin would be moved away from the coast. It made no difference whether or not they were US citizens.

At first, General DeWitt's military zones covered the western parts of Washington, Oregon, and California, and much of southern Arizona. The zones soon expanded to include the entire state of California. Japanese Americans were given a few weeks to leave the military zones voluntarily. About five thousand people seized this opportunity. They moved in with relatives who lived in Utah, Montana, or other inland states. However, most West Coast Japanese had nowhere to go. They could not make plans on such

Following evacuation orders, this store was closed. The owner, a University of California graduate of Japanese descent, had placed the "I Am An American" sign on the storefront the day after Pearl Harbor.

short notice. They stayed in their homes, hoping for the best. Voluntary relocation was ended on March 27, 1942.

A few weeks after Executive Order 9066 was announced, a curfew rule was imposed on the Japanese. All persons of Japanese heritage had to be in their homes between 8:00 p.m. and 6:00 a.m. During the day, they were forbidden to travel more than five miles from their homes or places of work.

The relocation process would be carried out by the Wartime Civil Control Administration under Colonel Karl Bendentsen. Bendentsen had worked closely with General DeWitt. He strongly believed that the Japanese Americans were a danger to national security. He was convinced that they should be removed from the coast until the war was over.

No one in the Japanese community knew how soon the evacuation orders would come. No one knew where they were going or how long they would be away. In the face of these uncertainties, the Japanese Americans prepared as best they could. Many families arranged for Caucasian friends or neighbors to store their furniture. Government warehouses were also available. However, the government warned that it could not be responsible for stored goods. Families who used government storage did so at their own risk.

Families rushed to sell the things they could not store quickly and safely. A woman from Washington State recalled:

> People came to buy things for nothing. We would have people come to the door, they'd want to buy the washing

Fighting Back

Not all of the Japanese Americans went along with the government's orders. Some broke the curfew. Some refused to register or to go to the camps. Minoru Yasui and Gordon Hirabayashi were among those arrested for disobeying the curfew rule and refusing to register. Fred Korematsu was jailed for remaining in a military zone after all Japanese Americans had been ordered to leave. These resisters claimed that the regulations violated their constitutional rights as American citizens. In a passionate statement, Gordon Hirabayashi proclaimed, "This order for the mass evacuation of all persons of Japanese descent denies them the right to live. . . . It kills the desire for a higher life. Hope for the future is exterminated."[20]

The Supreme Court heard the cases of United States of America v. Yasui and Hirabayashi v. United States in 1943. In 1944 it heard Korematsu v. United States. In all three cases the court upheld the curfew and relocation orders. It supported the power of the military above the constitutional rights of citizens during time of war. In the 1943 Yasui decision one of the justices wrote: "We cannot close our eyes to the fact . . . that, in time of war, residents having ethnic affiliations with an invading enemy may be a greater source of danger than those of a different ancestry."[21]

machine, the sewing machine, and they knew that we had to sell. And they would offer you a measly five dollars or something for something that we could still use.[22]

A college student named Yoshiko Uchida, whose father had been taken by the FBI, helped her mother sell the family's belongings. Years later, she wrote that in terrible haste: "[We] sold things we should have kept and packed away foolish trifles we should have discarded.[23]

People who ran farms or businesses were especially hard hit. Unless a trusted friend could take over, they were forced to sell off their assets. Farmers sold produce, equipment, and land for a fraction of their worth. Shopkeepers sold off their merchandise, taking whatever price they could get.

On bulletin boards and telephone poles from Washington to Arizona, notices began to appear. They announced that all people of Japanese heritage would have to register with the military. Soon after registration they would be relocated. It might be weeks later or within just a few days. The notices explained that each person could take only what she or he could carry in two suitcases. They should bring clothing, blankets, cups, and silverware. No pets would be allowed.

The "no pets" rule caused heartbreak to many Nisei children. They grieved at being parted from their beloved dogs and cats. One eight-year-old Washington girl remembered her desperate search for a home for her long-haired, plume-tailed little dog. At last, to her joy, a neighbor agreed to take care of him. "I took the dog over," she remembered, "and I had to be home by eight, so all we could do was hurry over, leave the dog, the blanket and the foods, and hurry home. Oh, that was a real sad thing. It was only a dog, but it was part of the family."[24]

Despite the wrenching losses, most of the Japanese made ready without protest. The JACL encouraged everyone to cooperate with the relocation orders. JACL leaders claimed that full cooperation would prove the loyalty of the Japanese Americans.

On the night before he and his family left to be relocated, a Washington farmer named Mutsuo Hashiguchi wrote an open letter to his local newspaper. Hashiguchi's letter reveals the spirit with which many Japanese Americans faced relocation. He wrote:

> Dear lifetime buddies, pals, and friends,
>
> With the greatest of regrets, we leave you for the duration, knowing deep in our hearts that when we return, we will be welcomed back . . . as neighbors. . . . There will be no trace of bitterness within our group, or any show of disrespect toward our government. . . . We accept the military order with good grace. We write this letter to thank the community for its past favors shown to us, the spirit of sportsmanship showered upon us, and the wholesome companionship afforded us. . . .
>
> Respectfully Yours,
> Mutsuo Hashiguchi.[25]

Camp Life

I was too young to understand, but I do remember . . . the sight of high guard towers . . . and I remember being afraid.

—Former detainee
George Takei[1]

After President Roosevelt signed Executive Order 9066, there was a rush to build accommodations for the Japanese Americans. It would take some time for the relocation camps to be ready, so temporary housing would have to be used in the interim. To meet this need, the military set up a series of assembly centers in California, Oregon, and Washington.

Sixteen-year-old Mary Matsuda never forgot her first glimpse of the Pinedale Assembly Center in the California desert. "Soldiers with machine guns stood in twenty-foot-high guard towers situated at strategic points along the perimeter of a huge camp," she wrote more than fifty years later. "The area was encased in steel wire fencing topped by three rows of barbed wire. Large searchlights next to the towers rotated continuously. . . . Impatient soldiers yelled at us to move forward, into the camp, as a stream of Japanese families flowed in behind us."[2]

In most cases, the army used racetracks and fairgrounds to house the relocated Japanese. Barracks were hammered together where Ferris wheels and roller coasters once stood. Horses were moved out of stables to make room for human occupants.

A Japanese-American man in San Francisco stands with his luggage as he waits to be taken to an internment camp.

Hiro Fugii, her husband, Masuji, and their infant son lived for four months in a horse stall at the Tanforan Racetrack near San Jose, California. The stall was about the size of a two-car garage. "The wall partitions didn't go all the way to the top. You could hear the people all up and down the row, and they could hear you," Mrs. Fugii recalled. "There was no privacy."[3]

Bad as these accommodations were, Hiro Fugii discovered that some were far worse. Her sister-in-law and two small children lived in a stall at the other end of the racetrack:

> They had linoleum on top of the floor, and the kids' clothes piled up in the middle. Around the edges there were a couple of inches where the linoleum did not reach, and there was a lot of brown liquid oozing because the linoleum had just been placed on top of the manure. I cried—it was just so sad![4]

Meals were served in large mess halls. Everyone waited in long lines in order to eat. When they finally filled their plates, the portions were small and the food starchy and dull. A doctor at Tanforan reported:

> [There is] no milk for any one over 5 years of age. . . . No meat at all until 12th day when very small portions were served. . . . Anyone doing heavy or outdoor work states they are not getting nearly enough to eat and they are hungry all the time. This includes the doctor.[5]

Japanese-American children say goodbye before leaving for an internment camp in the state of Washington.

A teenage boy, held at the Santa Anita Racetrack near Los Angeles, remembered, "One day I and some friends went to Mess Hall One and saw on a table reserved for doctors and nurses a lot of lettuce and tomatoes, fresh. We just went wild and grabbed at it like animals. . . . It was the best treat I ever had!"[6]

For many, lack of privacy was the hardest part of life in the assembly centers. The only bathrooms were public latrines. "The sink was a long metal trough against one wall, with a row of spigots for hot and cold water," wrote Jean Wakatsuke Houston, who was interned at Manzanar as a child. "Down the center of the room twelve toilet bowls were arranged in six pairs back to back, with no partitions. My mother was a very modest person, and this was going to be agony for her, sitting down in public, among strangers."[7] Some people collected sheets of cardboard from packing boxes. They carried the cardboard to the latrines and propped it around themselves when they sat on the toilet.

Mary Matsuda remembered being caught by the sweeping searchlight as she dashed to the latrine in the middle of the night. "In the darkness the searchlight had grabbed my privacy and exposed it to the camp guards. Blinded and stunned, I felt invaded. Powerless to stop the searchlight from bearing down on me, I fled back to the barracks."[8]

An officer reviews a list of items surrendered by a Japanese man prior to his internment.

Despite the miserable conditions, most of the Japanese Americans tried to make the best of their situation. People made friends at the mess halls and public laundry rooms. Some even planted vegetables and flowers in wooden boxes. By summer, morning glories began to climb stable walls, and chrysanthemums brightened tiny barracks gardens.[9] Then, in the early fall, the permanent internment camps were ready at last. It was time for the families to move again.

Dealing With Hardship

For the second time, Japanese Americans were herded onto trains. Again the shades were drawn, and again

Internees prepare lunch at the Santa Anita assembly center.

Relocating the Masses

Between 1942 and 1945, about 120,000 people lived in ten relocation centers on the US mainland. These included some 110,000 people forced from their homes on the West Coast, 1,275 people transferred to the centers from nursing homes and psychiatric institutions, 1,118 people relocated from Hawaii, 5,981 children born in the camps, and 219 non-Japanese who chose to accompany their Japanese spouses.[10] All of these people were held at ten internment camps: Tule Lake, California; Manzanar, California; Poston, Arizona; Gila River, Arizona; Topaz, Utah; Amache, Colorado (also known as Granada); Minidoka, Idaho; Heart Mountain, Wyoming; Jerome, Arkansas; and Rohwer, Arkansas.

In addition, as many as 7,000 Japanese Americans were arrested by the FBI early in the war and held at detention centers.[11] These centers included facilities at Santa Fe, New Mexico, and Missoula, Montana. Hundreds of people were held at New York's Ellis Island, once a processing center for new immigrants to the United States. At the largest detention center, near Crystal City, Texas, detainees could be joined by their families.

The Amache relocation center in Colorado held over seven thousand Japanese Americans from 1942 to 1945.

the evacuees did not know their destination. They only hoped it would be better than the assembly centers they were leaving behind.

The US government established ten relocation centers, also known as internment camps, for the Japanese Americans. All of the centers were in remote, desolate parts of the country. Eight stood on barren deserts. The other two were built in the swamps of Arkansas. "The heat, the freezing cold [at night], and the invasive dust storms told me that America had found a special hell for us," wrote Mary Matsuda, whose family was interned at Tule Lake Relocation Center in northern California. She asked herself, "What had we done to deserve this treatment?"[12]

In many ways, the internment camps resembled the assembly centers. Each camp was surrounded by a high barbed-wire fence. Again, armed soldiers kept watch from tall guard towers, and searchlights swept the grounds at night. However, here none of the internees had to live in horse stalls. Instead, everyone lived in barracks that were divided into tiny apartments. Some of the barracks were still under construction when the internees arrived. Even when finished, the buildings were poorly made. Roger Walker, a serviceman who worked at the Topaz Relocation Center in Utah, was appalled by the housing conditions. He recalled.

> The sheeting had cracks at least a quarter of an inch between each board. [There was] no insulation whatsoever. . . . There were bare [light] bulbs, eight to every hundred and twenty feet [of wire]. . . . Just one wire down the length and a switch over by the door. . . . There were no concrete foundations under the barracks. . . . It is really difficult to see how [the internees] survived."[13]

Dust was an endless problem in the desert camps. It filtered in through the cracks and sifted onto furniture, bedding, and food. No matter how often the internees swept, a layer of dust always seemed to cover everything. Sometimes high winds gathered the dust into thick, rushing clouds. These violent dust storms could be terrifying. A high school student remembered such a storm at Topaz: "There seemed to be a wall way out there; to see the blue sky and then the more you look at it, the wall seems to be moving. It was a dust storm rolling in, and it just engulfed you, and before you knew it, you could not see anything."[14]

Although the internees had never been accused of any crime, they were treated as if they were convicts. Even young children were handled as though they were dangerous enemy agents. Three-year-old John Tateishi came down with German measles as his family was on its way to Manzanar. He was taken to a nearby hospital and placed under quarantine. Years later, he recalled, "[I was] placed under armed guard because I was, after all, someone the United States government deemed 'dangerous' to the security of the country."[15]

Everyone was warned to stay a safe distance away from the fence. Anyone who ventured too close could be shot on sight. As a teenager at Topaz, Harry Kitano tried to test the limits. One day, he and his friends managed to slip out of camp. "The camp was located in the middle of a desert and there was virtually no place to go," Kitano remembered. "After walking about fifty yards past a break in the wire fence we were surrounded by military policemen with drawn guns, interrogated, our names recorded, loaded on jeeps, and returned to camp. It was a frightening and sobering experience."[16]

At Topaz, a sixty-three-year-old man named James Nakasa approached the fence one evening, apparently collecting pieces of scrap lumber. A guard fired, and Nakasa died instantly. Later the guard testified that Nakasa had been fleeing, trying to escape. To the

Dust was a problem at many of the camps, which were located in rugged terrain. In this photo by Dorothea Lange, a dust storm sweeps through this War Relocation Authority center in Manzanar, California.

internees at Topaz, the guard's story seemed unlikely. Nakasa was shot in the chest, not in the back.

Such tragic incidents were rare. Nevertheless, the constant presence of armed guards created a sense of fear. For many internees there were feelings of shame as well. They had been hardworking members of the community. Now they were being treated as if they were criminals. The experience was degrading and discouraging. John Tateishi was only seven when his family was interned at Manzanar. "We knew even then as kids that we carried the same guilt and shame our

A guard on duty at the camp at Manzanar.

parents felt," he wrote later. "They could not protect themselves, and worse, they could not protect us or hide the humiliation they were forced to endure."[17]

As they had at the assembly centers, most of the internees tried to come to peace with their situation. Often they turned to one another with the Japanese phrase, "*Shikata ga nai*," meaning, "It can't be helped." Tears and bitterness were of no use. Since they had to stay in the camps, they determined to build a life there.

Adjusting to a New Life

Each of the ten internment camps was like a small city. On average, the camps held about ten thousand people. Tule Lake, the largest, had a population of over eighteen thousand at its peak.[18] Because the camps were built in such remote places, they were usually the biggest population centers for miles around. With about fourteen thousand people the camp at Poston became the third largest city in Arizona.[19]

To run the internment camps, President Roosevelt created a new federal department called the War Relocation Authority (WRA). The first WRA director was Milton Eisenhower, brother to the army general and future president, Dwight D. Eisenhower. Milton Eisenhower had serious doubts about the internment plan. Later he wrote: "The President's final decision was influenced by a variety of factors—by events over which he had little control, by inaccurate or incomplete information, by bad counsel, by strong political pressures, and by his own training, background, and

Japanese Americans work at a store on the grounds of the Tule Lake camp.

personality."[20] Eisenhower resigned after holding the position for only a few weeks. His replacement, Dillon Myers, headed the WRA until the end of the war.

The WRA appointed a director and administrative staff for each of the camps. Nearly all of the camp administrators were Caucasians. However, the WRA tried to give the internees a role in governing the camps. A camp council consisted of elected representatives from each block. A block consisted of fourteen barracks, and held about three hundred people.

The block representatives brought their concerns and suggestions to the administration. They raised issues about many aspects of camp life. Their concerns included food, health care, schooling, and recreation. However, the councils had little real power. They could offer ideas, but they could seldom make binding decisions.

The internees sometimes grew to distrust members of the council. They called them by a Japanese word, *inu*, meaning "dogs." Inu were thought to be spies, carrying reports of unrest to the administration. Some internees believed that anyone who became friendly with Caucasian staff members, even with teachers or nurses, was probably a spy.

Camp life fell into a steady routine. Three times a day the mess-hall bell rang out, calling the internees to meals. The bell also announced block meetings and other gatherings. The clanging of the bell marked the slow passing of the days.

In some cases, the government hired Caucasian teachers, doctors, nurses, and other professionals

Students attend school at the Tule Lake relocation center.

to work in the camps. In addition, some qualified internees took these positions. In this way, the internees helped build the services they needed. They taught school, cared for the sick, and even policed the camp's grounds. Internees with an interest in writing ran camp newspapers. Musicians put on shows in the camp's recreation centers. Internees served as cooks and dishwashers and ran stores on the camp's grounds.

Internee workers were paid for their labor by the government. Depending on the job, they received $13, $16, or $19 per month. This pay scale was extremely low, even for the early 1940s. Yoriyuki Kikuchi, an Issei dentist, earned $19 a month at Manzanar. On the outside, before his internment, he earned about $300 a month.[21]

When they were not working, the internees found ways to enjoy life. They visited their neighbors and exchanged bits of camp news. Internees at Topaz created a series of ponds, landscaped with rocks and fountains. At Tule Lake and some other desert camps, people collected tiny fossil shells. They made the shells into beautiful pieces of jewelry. Women in the camps attended classes to learn English and such crafts as quilting and ceramics. Many of the Issei women were thrilled to have these opportunities. For the first time in their lives they were free from household chores. At last they could pursue interests outside the home.[22]

Children and teens found delight in many aspects of camp life. Children played tag and hide-and-seek from barrack to barrack. Teens enjoyed Saturday night dances. Instead of sitting with their parents in the mess halls, they drifted away to eat with their friends. They fashioned a world of their own, free from adult interference. Their parents were distressed by the fraying of family ties. They worried that their children had too much freedom. Many parents tried to lay down rules as they had at home. However, in camp the old ways no longer applied. Camp life had its own rules.

Though the children and teens enjoyed their freedom within the camps, they could never forget the guard towers and searchlights. The fence surrounded them, holding them prisoner inside. There was no break in the endless routine, no chance to touch the world outside. A twelve-year-old boy's essay in a

Images of Despair

Among the employees of the WRA were several talented photographers. These men and women took pictures of the evacuees on transport trains, in assembly centers, and finally in the internment camps. The most famous internment photographers were Ansel Adams and Dorothea Lange. For the most part, the internees welcomed the photographers. They were glad that their story would be captured on film for the world to see. The photographers were generally sympathetic toward the Japanese Americans. Dorothea Lange later wrote that the internment was "an example of what happens to us if we lose our heads. . . . What was of course horrifying was to do this thing completely on the basis of what blood may be coursing through a person's veins, nothing else."[23]

Ansel Adams took this photo from a guard tower of the internment camp at Manzanar in the summer of 1943.

Children interned at Tule Lake play a game.

Manzanar camp magazine conveys his longing for an ordinary family vacation:

> Last week my family and I started by car on a trip to Death Valley. Leaving the car, part of our trip was made on horseback. We saw many pretty wild flowers and bushes. We saw the mystic sand dunes and found some strange ruins. Everything looked so strange and beautiful that I felt like taking the whole desert home with me and showing it to everyone I met. . . . We had to spend the night on the lonely desert with the stars and the sky overhead. It grew windy, but finally we slept. Then morning came and where do you think we were?—In our own beds! This was only a dream.[24]

A Way Out

Within the camps there was a diverse group of people from all walks of life. "Mostly we all got along in camp," recalled Hiro Fugii of her experience at Topaz. "We were all in the same boat, you see. It made us all the same."[1] While most people did their best to co-exist peacefully with their neighbors, some conflict was unavoidable.

People from many different backgrounds lived side-by-side in the camps. Doctors and teachers waited in line at the mess hall behind farmers and fishermen. Educated people sometimes resented living so close to members of the working class. At the same time, some farmworkers and fishers thought that the educated internees were snobbish.

Sue Kunitomi's family was financially comfortable before internment. At Manzanar, Sue was exposed for the first time to other elements of society. She was afraid of the people who came from San Pedro Island off the California coast. "The San Pedro people were kind of rough," she recalled. "They were fishermen and they lived in their little ingrown community in San Pedro and Terminal Island, and they were almost like a Japanese village.[2] During a baseball game at camp, some San Pedro players felt they had been insulted. After the game, they roved from barrack to barrack, picking fights with members of the opposing team.

Camp life also caused tension between the older and younger generations. By Japanese tradition, older persons were deeply respected by the young. In some ways, camp life turned this tradition on its head. Because they were US citizens, the Nisei were given greater privileges than their Japanese-born parents. Nisei ran the camp councils and held the most valued jobs. The Issei often felt pushed aside by their own children. George Fukasawa, a Nisei photographer, told an interviewer, "The Issei man who tradition-ally headed the family found that . . . he didn't have a family anymore. And I think that was the biggest blow to them."[3]

In some camps, political differences created deep divisions. The Japanese American Citizens League (JACL) encouraged internees to cooperate with the white administration. It urged the internees to prove their patriotism by following camp rules. Some internees resented the JACL and opposed its approach. They felt that the Japanese Americans were being mistreated by the US government. These people, mostly young Nisei men, sometimes stirred rebellious

In the internment camps, older people often received less respect than US-born Japanese Americans.

Divided Loyalties

Protest against the camp authorities most often came from a group of Japanese Americans called the Kibei. The Kibei were Nisei who had been educated in Japan. Issei parents often sent their American-born children (especially their sons) to attend school in Japan for several years. In this way, the Kibei became fluent in the Japanese language. Many also adopted the pro-military thinking that arose in Japan during the prewar years. When they returned to the United States, the Kibei tended to have strong loyalties to Japan. Although they were American citizens, they felt that they were foreigners in the United States.

feelings within the camps. At times, conflicts flared between the rebels and the JACL and its allies.

Fred Tayama was a leader of the JACL at Manzanar. On the night of December 6, 1942, he was brutally beaten by six men. Badly injured, Tayama was rushed to the camp hospital. He told camp officials he did not know who his attackers were. The following day, camp police arrested Harry Ueno, a worker in the camp kitchen. No evidence linked Ueno to the attack on Tayama. However, he had often criticized how the camp was run. He had recently accused camp officials of stealing sugar and meat that were intended for the internees.

Hundreds of internees protested Ueno's arrest. Some threatened violence against JACL members. "I remember hearing the crowds rush past our block that night," wrote Jean Wakatsuke Houston. "Toward the end of it they were a lynch mob, swarming from one side of the camp to the other, from the hospital to the police station to the barracks of the men they were after, shouting slogans in English and Japanese."[4] The mob broke into the hospital, intending to murder Tayama. He managed to escape by hiding under a bed. Camp officials called in the military police to break up the crowds. Some reports claim that protesters threw rocks at the police.

Finally the police fired into the crowd of unarmed protesters. Two internees were killed and ten more were wounded. The incident, known as the Manzanar Riot, was the worst outbreak of violence in the relocation camps.

News of the Manzanar Riot sped from one camp to another. Internees wondered whether violence would erupt in other camps as well. Then, in January 1943, they were caught up in a fresh upheaval.

Yes or No?

In the winter of 1943, the WRA distributed a questionnaire throughout the ten relocation camps. All internees age seventeen and over were required to complete the form. Most of the questions were simple and straightforward. Questions 27 and 28, however,

Clash at Tule Lake

Many of the internees at Tule Lake raised and harvested vegetables to feed the camp. Late in 1943, these laborers went on strike, calling for better working conditions. For the most part the strike was peaceful. However, in one incident internees clashed with camp security officers. One officer and several internees were injured. The press called this incident the Tule Lake Riot. Some newspapers used it to heighten the public's mistrust of Japanese Americans. The *New York Times* stated: "We can't give leeway to possible spies and saboteurs simply because we want to believe that human nature, including that which is wrapped in a saffron-colored skin, is inherently good."[5]

posed problems for many Issei and Nisei. Question 27 asked male internees: "Are you willing to serve in the armed services in combat duty, wherever ordered?" The questionnaire asked women if they would be willing to serve with the US military as nurses. Question 28 read: "Will you swear unqualified allegiance to the United States of America, and faithfully defend the United States from any or all attack by foreign or domestic forces, and forswear any form of allegiance or obedience to the Japanese emperor or any other foreign government, power, or organization?"

The WRA hoped to move as many internees as possible out of the camps and return them to life on the outside. Japanese Americans would not be allowed to go back to the West Coast, but they could be resettled in the central and eastern parts of the country. Before they could leave the camps, however, the internees had to declare their loyalty to the United States. The WRA designed the questionnaire with this purpose in mind.

The questionnaire sparked fierce debate among the internees. Some felt it was their patriotic duty to answer yes to both questions 27 and 28. They believed they should defend the United States, even though it had imprisoned them and their families. Others felt just as strongly that they should refuse to defend the United States in a war. The United States had treated them as enemies. They felt they did not owe it their allegiance unless it reinstated their rights as citizens. Question 28 posed special problems for the Issei. The Issei had never been allowed to become citizens of

Members of the WRA hold a meeting with Japanese-American representatives at Tule Lake.

the United States. If they gave up their allegiance to Japan, they would belong to no country at all.

For weeks, people in the camps struggled over the questionnaires. What would happen, they asked one another, to people who answered no to questions 27 and 28? Would they be sent away to a detention camp such as Crystal City? If a young man answered yes to both questions, did that mean he would have to join the army? And suppose someone answered yes to 27 but no to 28? How would the authorities handle that?

Mary Matsuda argued with herself long and hard before she decided how she would answer. In her heart she did not want to answer yes to questions 27 and 28.

She did not want to promise service and allegiance to the country that had locked her family behind barbed wire. Yet her parents and her brother had answered yes to both questions. If she answered no and no, perhaps she would be separated from her family. She imagined the wrenching moment of parting:

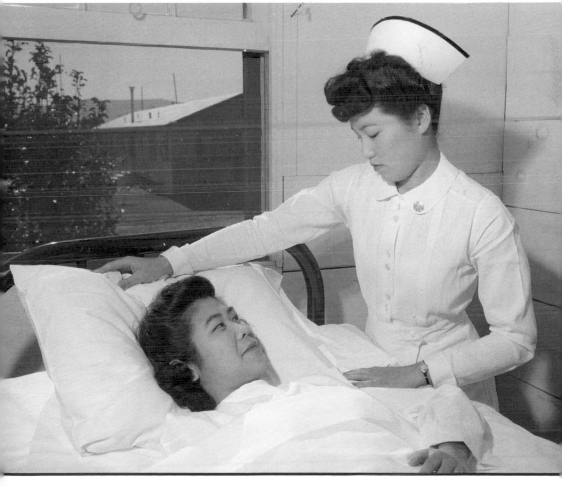

A nurse cares for a patient at the Manzanar Relocation Center in 1943.

Dinner is served cafeteria-style in the mess halls at the Heart Mountain Relocation Center in California.

I pictured myself standing alone outside their railroad car. . . . When the "All aboard!" rang out and the train slowly started to move, I wondered when or if I would see them again. With that thought clawing at my heart, the tears would well up in my eyes. I saw myself walking slowly at first keeping pace with the moving car, my tears flowing, then striding more vigorously as the train picked up speed, until I could no longer keep up. With an overwhelming sense of loss and pain, I would stagger to a stop and watch the train leave the station, taking my family away from me.[6]

To remain with her family Mary answered yes to both of the troubling questions on the form.

WRA officials were shocked and dismayed by the reaction to the questionnaire. They had not expected people to be so distressed. They made some changes to the critical questions, hoping to ease the minds of the internees. The changes came too late to be of much help. Debate over the WRA questionnaire created terrible divisions within the camps. Friendships shattered and neighbors hurled accusations at neighbors. Questions 27 and 28 even caused rifts within families—between parents and children, brothers and sisters, husbands and wives.

In the end, about three thousand people refused to complete the questionnaire. Some seventy-five thousand people filled out the form as the WRA required. Of these, 6,700 answered no to Question #28.[7] Many of the people who answered no to both questions were young men. They came to be known as the "no-no boys."

The internees who answered yes to questions 27 and 28 could apply to leave the camps to work or attend college. Those who answered no or who refused to complete the questionnaire were moved to the camp at Tule Lake. "Yes-yes" internees already living at Tule Lake were offered the chance to transfer to another camp. Many of them did so. Tule Lake became known as a camp for rebels and troublemakers.

Once the no-no internees were moved to Tule Lake, the WRA put the next stage of its plan into motion. It began encouraging the yes-yes internees to leave the camps.

Exit Plans

"A [place], or you might have called it a corral, like Manzanar [had] no exit save via three narrow gates," wrote Jean Wakatsuke Houston. "The first led into the infantry, the second back across the Pacific. The third, called *relocation*, was just opening up."[8] From the time it was established, the War Relocation Authority hoped to move the Japanese Americans quickly out of the internment camps. While the war raged, however, they would not be allowed to return to the West Coast. As Houston explained, there were three options. Some internees left to join the US military. A few chose to return to Japan. The largest number who left the camps during the war years were relocated to cities and towns far from the Pacific shores.

In January 1943, the US Army announced the formation of an all-Nisei regiment, the 442nd Regimental Combat Team. Nisei from Hawaii had already been serving as the 100th Battalion. The 100th Battalion and the 442nd Regiment became a combined fighting unit.

Many Nisei joined the 442nd because military service gave them a way to leave the camps. In addition, they believed that going to war would help them prove their loyalty to the United States. By serving bravely, they hoped to overcome the shame of suspicion and internment.

About 18,500 Nisei men served in Europe as part of the 100th/442nd during World War II. The Nisei soldiers fought with extrardinary bravery and suffered

Fighting Words

As its slogan, the 442nd Regiment took the phrase, Go for Broke! The phrase came from a dice game that was popular with the Hawaiian Japanese. When a player decided to "go for broke," it meant that he or she risked everything.

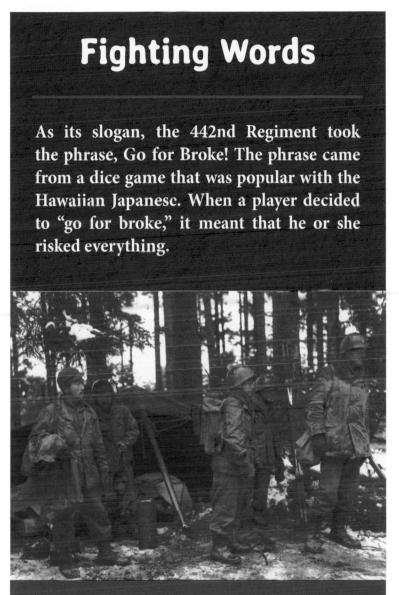

Members of the 442nd Combat Team, a Japanese-American fighting unit. Many men joined the military as a way of escaping the internment camps.

terrible losses. Their valor earned the soldiers many awards, including 9,486 Purple Hearts, 585 Silver Stars, and one Congressional Medal of Honor.[9]

Early in the war, the US government offered the Issei and Nisei the chance to move to Japan. A diplomatic arrangement with the Japanese government allowed some Japanese Americans to go back to their homeland. About seven thousand chose to accept this option. Others chose to move to Japan when the war was over. Some of these people felt strong ties of loyalty to Japan. Others were simply disheartened by their treatment in the United States. One Nisei woman explained, "I have American citizenship. It's no good, so what's the use? . . . I feel that we're not wanted in this country any longer. . . . It's too late for me, but at least [in Japan] I can bring up my children so that they won't have to face the same kind of trouble I've experienced."[10]

The third option offered to the internees during the war was relocation to an area away from the West Coast. Some forty-three hundred young people left the camps to attend college. Volunteer and charitable organizations provided them with scholarships and other assistance. The American Friends Service Committee (AFSC) played a leading role in helping students leave the camps.

Like the Nisei soldiers, most of the students felt they had been given a chance to prove that they were good American citizens. "It was a thrill to get accustomed to being 'free,'" wrote a boy who enrolled at the University of Colorado. "I think most of us realize our

A Japanese-American man transplants celery at Tule Lake. Some internees were allowed to leave the camps to help at other farms.

most important mission of being 'good-will ambassadors,' and to show other Americans that we are also loyal Americans."[11] The students tried to put whites at ease and not to call undue attention to themselves. They refrained from speaking Japanese with Nisei friends on campus. When they went shopping in town they avoided going with other Nisei. They sensed that Caucasians might find a group of Nisei threatening.

Dishonored Veterans

Thousands of Japanese fought bravely for the United States in World War II. In the small town of Hood River, Oregon, however, a group of veterans were treated with such disrespect that it attracted the attention of the entire nation. In early 1945 the names of sixteen Japanese-American veterans were removed from the honor roll at the local American Legion post. The leaders responsible claimed that they could not be certain of these veterans' loyalty to the United States. Given the fact that these men had fought, and in some cases died, for their country, it seemed outrageous to question their allegiance.

Word spread about the removal of the names. National publications like *Life* magazine ran stories about Hood River. The blatant racism and hatred displayed by this small group outraged much of the country. Within six weeks, the national head of the American Legion ordered that the names be restored. The damage was done, however, and fewer than half of the town's Japanese-American population chose to return to Hood River after the war.[12]

With so many young men away at war, farmhands were sorely needed to tend and harvest the nation's crops. The WRA urged internees to leave camp for work in the fields. Many of the Japanese Americans were experienced farmers. They welcomed the chance to leave camp and to do useful work again. Besides, as farmworkers they earned more than they could earn from jobs in the camps.

The internees proved to be invaluable workers. "If it had not been for Japanese labor," declared one official in Utah, "much of the [sugar] beet crop in Utah and Idaho would have been plowed up. . . . These are industrious people who want work."[13]

Early in the war, the internee workers left camp on temporary work leaves. When the crops were harvested they returned to camp. Later, they were encouraged to find work and remain on the outside. Some sprang at the chance, but others were reluctant. Those who had run into bad treatment on the outside sometimes preferred to stay in camp. A young man from Manzanar reported, "They refused us admittance to the movies; we couldn't get a meal at the cafes. They had a sign: 'NO JAPS!' We had to spend a night in jail, there was no other place to go."[14] After his months on the outside, Manzanar seemed like a safe haven.

As time passed, more and more internees left camp to work or study. Yet tens of thousands of people still remained interned. The majority were old people and mothers with children. As the war ground to a close, they wondered what the future held in store.

The Opening of the Gates

In 1944 World War II was slowly coming to an end. Japan's forces were weakening and the United States no longer feared an attack on the West Coast. The country's leaders had no reason to hold the Japanese Americans. "I have been talking to a number of people from the [West] Coast," wrote President Roosevelt that June, "and they are all in agreement that the Coast would be willing to receive back a portion of the Japanese who were once there—nothing sudden, and not in too great quantities at any one time."[1]

The question was where the internees should go when they left the camps. Officials feared that whites on the West Coast would be hostile toward their return. Even in other parts of the country the public would object to the arrival of large groups of former internees. After all, American soldiers were still fighting and dying in the Pacific. Japan was an enemy nation. Many Americans still connected the Japanese

Americans with the actions of their mother country. Roosevelt hoped that the Japanese Americans could be sent in small groups to cities and towns throughout the United States. As he put it, "I am sure that there would be no bitterness if they were distributed one or two families to each county as a start."[2]

Leaving the camps called for courage and will. Some people who had left reported harsh conditions in the world outside. They claimed that many Caucasians were unfriendly. Jobs were hard to come by, they said, and housing was scarce. Many of the people still living in the camps were afraid to venture out. A man at Topaz explained, "Here, there is little freedom; but we

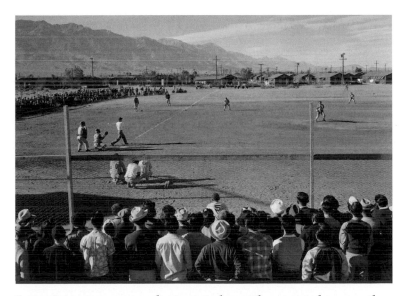

Some internees were reluctant to leave the camps because they had created a life there, and the outside world seemed uncertain. Above, internees play baseball at the camp in Manzanar, California, in this 1943 photo by Ansel Adams.

are not stared at. We do not get what we want here, but we live anyway and do not feel lonely."[3]

Every camp was a hotbed of rumors about life outside. At Tule Lake the rumors were especially frightening. Pro-Japanese gangs terrorized internees who were neutral or loyal to the United States. Gang members planted and spread rumors about the perils of leaving the camp. They told their fellow internees that Japanese Americans were being beaten and murdered. The only safety, they warned, was to stay in camp or to return to Japan.

Pressured by these gangs, many Tule Lake Issei asked the US government to send them back to their homeland. They also persuaded their Nisei children to renounce, or give up, their American citizenship. In

Some internees, like these at Tule Lake, worried about what would happen to them when they left the camp.

this way, desperate parents thought the family could stay together.

Eventually most of the rumors proved false. Many of the Issei changed their minds about returning to Japan. Most of the Nisei regretted renouncing their US citizenship. However, the government would not let them change their minds. In a letter to the Justice Department, one man explained that his wife had renounced her citizenship out of terrible fear. He pleaded:

> Do you know what it means, in a few minutes of hysteria to throw away your happiness, your family, your future, seemingly forever? . . . isn't there some way we can go out? Even if my wife's citizenship is gone . . . She did not renounce out of disloyalty. . . . She only wants us to be together. Isn't there some way by which our little family can relocate? Don't you see how awful our situation is? Do help us if you can![4]

The US Justice Department spent years examining the cases of Nisei who renounced their citizenship. In the end, it ruled ["reluctantly"] that "renunciations made behind barbed wire were essentially under duress."[5] Therefore, few of the Tule Lake internees were held to their renunciation decisions.

By 1945, most of the remaining internees were used to life in the camps. They knew what to expect from day to day. They went to meals when they heard the mess-hall bells. Their gardens and friendships made life bearable. The thought of the outside world reminded them of all they had lost. An Issei woman at Minidoka wrote:

> Some people hesitate to go back to their old home right away. And some ones don't know what to do, because they sold their property, furnitures, automobiles, etc., even their farm land and they have no places to go back now. The other day one of my neighbours told me "I don't want to take a risk, so I shall stay in this unpleasant camp till the war is over."[6]

Whether or not the internees were ready to leave, the WRA was determined to close the camps. Officials urged the internees to join friends and relatives outside. Then, in August 1945, the camps rocked with shocking news. The United States had dropped atomic bombs on the cities of Hiroshima and Nagasaki in Japan.

Saying Good-Bye

Most of the internees were horrified by the destruction of Hiroshima and Nagasaki. Many wept for relatives and old friends who had died in the bombings. Yet most were relieved to know that the war would soon be over. On August 14, Japan announced that it would surrender. The ceremony of surrender took place on September 2. The terrible fighting in the Pacific was finally at an end.

At the close of the war, some forty-four thousand people were still living in the ten internment camps. They comprised about one third of all those who had been interned.[7] Officials at each camp posted a schedule for closing. Each of the internees was given twenty-five dollars and a train ticket. Usually the

A man stands on top of a bus loading luggage while a group of people gather to say farewell at the Manzanar camp in 1943.

ticket would take the internee back to the town he or she left when internment began.

On March 20, 1946, the last internees—554 people—left Tule Lake. Many of them still were not free. Among them were some who had renounced their American citizenship or who had challenged the camp authorities. They were sent from Tule Lake to detention centers, such as Santa Fe or Crystal City. A government official reported on Tule Lake's final day:

> The day of closure had all the dramatic touches which marked the beginning of segregation. There were . . . the tearful partings and distraught people, . . .the same last-minute rush to the relocation bus, and, as always at Tule, the same inevitable waves of rumors. . . . Armed guards were swarming, search and seizure of forbidden articles were conducted.[8]

A few internees simply could not bear to face the outside world. They had to be forced out of the camps. One elderly Issei man, interned at Minidoka, refused to board the train for Seattle. He threw his twenty-five dollars on the ground and walked all the way back to the abandoned camp. Officials returned him to the station and put him forcibly onto a train.[9] The offices of the War Relocation Authority closed forever on June 30, 1946. For more than four years the WRA had managed the ten relocation camps and the lives of more than one hundred ten thousand people. Now, as the camp survivors began the slow process of rebuilding their lives, the WRA set its responsibilities aside. The agency's final report stated, "the obligation of the Federal Government to the evacuees has . . . been adequately discharged."[10]

By the summer of 1946, all of the camps were empty. Power and water were shut off. The mess hall bells fell silent. The wind whipped among the deserted barracks, carrying endless clouds of dust. No one was left to sweep it away. It settled on rooftops and sifted over gardens. It buried abandoned tools and forgotten toys. Little by little, it hid the last traces of the human stories that had played out on this patch of barren ground.

Going Home

In January 1945, the mayor of Los Angeles attended a special ceremony. The ceremony welcomed a group of returning Japanese Americans. "We want you and all

A man and his child return to their orchard in 1945 after leaving an internment camp.

other citizens of Japanese ancestry who have relocated here to feel secure in your home," the mayor declared.

People did not always meet such a welcome when they left the camps. Many Caucasians still feared and resented the Japanese. They did not want the Japanese Americans to move back to their old neighborhoods. Anti-Japanese organizations fanned their fears. "They [the Japanese Americans] didn't build us up," stated the newsletter of the Japanese Exclusion League in 1945. "They tore us down. We want no more of them."[11]

Dreading a hostile greeting on the coast, many Japanese Americans decided to settle in the East or the Midwest. Often they joined friends or relatives who had settled there when they left camp earlier. Away

A Japanese family returns to Seattle, Washington, from a relocation center camp in Hunt, Idaho, to find their home and garage with anti-Japanese graffiti and broken windows.

from the West Coast, they found little anti-Japanese feeling. A Nisei student in New York City explained: "The color of my skin and the slant of my eyes do not close doors upon me. . . . Draftsmen are working as draftsmen, engineers as engineers, teachers as teachers. Fruit stands are no longer the ultimate end of every [Japanese] college graduate."[12]

Nevertheless, most Japanese Americans thought of the West Coast as their true home. Many longed to return, in spite of their losses and fears. Tomoye Takahashi, a young mother interned at Topaz, yearned to go back to her native San Francisco. At last, after more than three years, she crossed San Francisco Bay on the ferry at sunset. "In the sky ahead of us, lavender was sliding into pearly gray and the tinted pinks and oranges couldn't have been more beautiful," she remembered. "I just stood there and wept. It was the greatest happening; I was finally coming home."[13]

Some of the former internees were fortunate. Friends and neighbors had taken good care of their homes and property. The former internees were able to move in and pick up the pieces of their lives. Others, however, found their houses burned or torn down. Some discovered that vandals had broken into their homes. The Hashiguchi family from Washington State found their farmhouse in a shambles. "It looked like the cows and pigs and everybody had walked in and out," Mitsuko Hashiguchi recalled. "Filthy, and the main part is, we didn't have any water, because the well was all filled with all kinds of junk. Everything you could think of was in that." The family's storage room had

These ranchers are signing a petition to boycott Japanese businesses. Returning Japanese Americans often faced this type of discrimination after the war.

been raided, and most of their belongings were broken or missing. Mitsuko Hashiguchi explained, "American friends told me [that] the day we moved out, [the looters] came in truckloads and just cleaned out all the Japanese homes, anything they could get into."[14]

The US government did little to help the former internees who faced such losses. Some church groups pitched in, and friends and neighbors offered what assistance they could. In general, the public was sympathetic toward the families leaving the camps. The bitterness of the early war years was melting away.

Perhaps the greatest force in changing public opinion was the heroism of the 442nd Regiment. The young men who volunteered to serve their country had proven what they set out to prove. They had shown that they were loyal citizens of the United States. As they bled and died, they redeemed the honor of their families and their race.

Homes in Ruins

By the beginning of 1945, a scattering of internees had returned to their homes on the West Coast. Although most resettled peacefully, some ran into serious trouble. The story of the Doi family confirmed the fears of those still in camp.

Shortly after the Doi family returned to their farm in Placer County, California, vandals set fire to a shed on their property. Then someone fired shots at the house. A group of soldiers and local women confessed to the attack. The attackers were tried and acquitted by a jury. Altogether about thirty incidents of harassment and vandalism against Japanese Americans were reported in 1945 and 1946. These included the burning of ten Japanese homes.[15]

Early in 1946, veterans of the 442nd marched smartly down Constitution Avenue in Washington, DC. In a formal ceremony, President Harry S. Truman awarded the Distinguished Unit Citation to the 442nd Regiment. "You fought for the free nations of the world with the rest of us," Truman declared. "I congratulate you on that, and I can't tell you how very much the United States of America thinks of what you have done. You are now on your way home. You fought not only the enemy but you fought prejudice and you have won."[16]

The Japanese Americans had faced internment with quiet acceptance. Now, with the same steady

Members of the 442nd regiment receive citations for bravery.

The Price of Internment

Internment caused the Japanese Americans to suffer massive financial losses. It was hard to attach a cost in dollars to the loss of homes and businesses. It was impossible to put a price on shattered dreams, fractured family life, and broken spirits. The Federal Reserve Bank of San Francisco estimated that the internees suffered losses totaling 400 million dollars. In 1948 President Truman signed the Japanese American Evacuation Claims Act in an effort to compensate the former internees. Congress allotted only 38 million dollars to be shared among the people who had been evacuated. Even then, each individual claim had to be examined and argued in the courts. The process of compensation was long and frustrating. The last claim was not settled until 1964. Altogether 38 million dollars was divided among 26,560 claimants.[17]

calm, they set about to rebuild their lives. On his way to Manzanar in 1942, Yoriyuki Kikuchi, an Issei dentist, saw a pile of uprooted geranium plants. The flowers reminded him of the undefeatable spirit of the evacuees.

They had been uprooted and tossed beside the road. Some day they would rise and bloom again.[18]

Chapter 7

Rebuilding Dreams

I still believe in our American way of life. After the camps . . . I fought for the kind of country I would like for it to be. . . . I [became] active in fights against discrimination and fights for justice.

—Former detainee Chizu Iiyama[1]

In the years following World War II, the internment camp survivors picked up the pieces of their lives and began again. Despite everything the United States had put them through during the war, they were still determined to make it their home. Then in 1952 they received long overdue news. Congress had passed the McCarran-Walter Act, finally granting Asian immigrants the right to become American citizens.

Mary Matsuda's father and mother stood before a judge in 1954 and promised to be loyal citizens of the United States. After decades in the United States, the Matsudas were naturalized citizens at last. "It was the fulfillment of their lifelong dream," their daughter wrote. "Even though it took them so many years, it gave them great satisfaction and a sense that all of their sacrifice had been worth it."[2]

Across America, the former internees worked hard, saved money, and bought homes. They encouraged their children to do well in school. The third generation of Japanese Americans, known as the *Sansei*, entered business and the professions. Anti-Asian discrimination had held their parents back. Now much of that discrimination was fading. Young Sansei were free to choose among a host of sparkling opportunities.

Most of the Issei and Nisei tried to put internment far behind them. They did not want to talk about the years they had spent behind fences. Many parents did not even tell their children what had happened to them. A cloak of silence covered their anger, hurt, and shame.

Jeni Yamada was eleven in 1962 when a story on the evening news caught her attention. A newsclip showed armed soldiers herding Japanese Americans onto a train. The newscaster explained that, twenty years ago, Japanese Americans had been relocated from Los Angeles to Manzanar. Jeni was shocked when she learned that her own mother had been interned. "Mom," she asked, "how come you never told us?"[3]

Jeni's mother, Mitsuye Yamada, had wanted to keep her painful story of internment from her children. She had believed that she could protect them by hiding

In 1952, a group of men celebrate the passing of the McCarran–Walter Act, which permitted Japanese immigrants to become naturalized citizens of the United States. Each person writes their thoughts on the important event.

the past. Jeni's question helped her realize that silence caused its own kind of harm. Jeni had a right to know the history of her family and her people.

During the 1960s and 1970s, the children of former internees began to ask questions. With their prodding, parents and grandparents broke their long silence. For the first time, they told stories of horse stalls, watch towers, and mess halls. They spoke of their sense of loss and betrayal and described their struggle to start anew.

Once the silence was broken, Mitsuye Yamada and many others shared their stories with the public. Some captured their experiences in poetry and memoirs. Some spoke about internment with historians. Former internees, with their children and friends, sought ways to honor the innocent thousands who had been imprisoned. They wanted to be sure that the story of the internment would never be forgotten. By reminding the world of what had happened, they hoped that such a tragedy would never occur again.

A group of Issei prepare for a sightseeing tour shortly after becoming American citizens in 1956.

Clearing Their Names

During the 1980s, Minoru Yasui, Gordon Hirabayashi, and Fred Korematsu reopened their court cases from forty years before. Their appeals were filed as "petitions of coram nobis." *Coram nobis* is a legal term that means "error before us." It can be used if a person believes that a legal error led to his or her conviction.

Minoru Yasui's petition was rejected by the courts. However, the rulings in Hirabayashi's and Korematsu's cases were overturned. In Hirabayashi's case, a judge ruled that the War Department had committed "an error of the most fundamental character."[4] In their final years these two men saw their names cleared.

On a windy day in December 1973 some fifteen hundred people gathered at the abandoned Manzanar camp. The crowd came to dedicate Manzanar as a California Historic Landmark. The visitors found few traces of the community that had survived for more than three years in the desert. Many of the flimsy barracks had tumbled into ruins. Only the stone guardhouse stood sturdy and immovable.

As the crowd looked on, a stonemason carefully set a bronze plaque into the guardhouse wall. The inscription on the plaque read:

> In the early part of World War II, 110,000 persons of Japanese ancestry were interned in relocation centers by Executive Order 9066 issued on February 19, 1942. Manzanar, the first of ten such concentration camps, was bounded by barbed wire and guard towers, confining 10,000 persons, the majority being American citizens. May the injustices and humiliation suffered here as a result of hysteria, racism and economic exploitation never emerge again.[5]

Demanding Justice

The movement began slowly—a suggestion here, a discussion there, somewhere else a heated debate. More and more Japanese Americans voiced the belief that they should receive payment from the federal government. The payment would not be a direct compensation for what they had lost. Rather, it would be a form of apology from the US government toward the people whom it had wronged. Such a payment is known as a restitution, or redress.

The redress movement gathered force during the 1970s. Several Japanese-American organizations worked to move a redress bill through Congress. Among these organizations was the Japanese American Citizens League (JACL). In 1980 Congress appointed the Commission on Wartime Relocation and Internment of Civilians (CWRIC). The commission studied records and held a series of public hearings. In 1983, it released its findings in a final report. The report was entitled *Personal Justice Denied*. "Executive Order 9066 was not justified by military necessity," the report stated. It continued:

> ...and the decisions that followed from it—exclusion, detention, the ending of detention and the ending of exclusion—were not founded upon military consider-ations. The broad historical causes that shaped these decisions were race prejudice, war hysteria, and a failure of political leadership.[6]

The Commission went on to recommend a program of redress of internment camp survivors.

Some Americans strongly opposed the redress movement. They claimed that Japan had been cruel to its prisoners of war during World War II. The United States had been far kinder to the internees. Why, then, should the United States pay restitution to the Japanese Americans? Opponents of redress argued that the US government had done what it thought best to protect the country. However, as stories of the internment came to light, the public grew sympathetic toward the former internees. Most Americans agreed with the CWRIC that the United States had committed a grave injustice against some of its own people. The intern-ment violated the most basic rights of Americans as stated in the US Constitution.

On August 10, 1988, a new law was passed in Congress. The Civil Liberties Act of 1988 called for

Japanese-American families, like the one shown here, often lost their livelihoods as a result of internment. Decades after the war, Japanese Americans began to demand retribution for both emotional and financial losses.

twenty thousand dollars to be sent to each person who had been interned. About half of the former internees were still alive on the day the bill was signed into law.

Learning From the Past

Most Americans who are old enough can describe exactly what they were doing when they learned that Japanese planes had bombed Pearl Harbor. They can tell you what they thought and felt when the news

President Bill Clinton presents Fred Korematsu with a Presidential Medal of Freedom during a ceremony at the White House on January 15, 1998. Korematsu's legal challenges to civilian exclusion orders during World War II helped spur the redress movement for Japanese Americans.

broke. Until their last breaths, Pearl Harbor day will be stamped upon their memories.

In much the same way, Americans will always remember where they were on the morning of September 11, 2001. They can describe how they put aside work or study or packing for a trip, to sit in horror before the television. Terrorists had flown jet planes into the World Trade Center and the Pentagon. Would there be more attacks, people wondered. Would the world ever feel safe again?

For Japanese-American internment survivors, 9/11 had special meaning. The surprise attacks reawakened memories of Pearl Harbor and its aftermath. Japanese Americans recalled the hostility they faced at the outbreak of World War II. "I didn't have any bad dreams, but it surely brought up bad memories," explained Tosh Ito, a former internee. "There was a lot of mass hysteria, a lot of discrimination, and it was not subtle at all. It was right out there. . . . [In later years] I think some of us thought it was pretty much gone. But 9/11 brought all of it out again."[7]

After 9/11, some camp survivors wondered what would happen to Americans of Arab descent. Would they be arrested and interned because a small group of Arabs had staged the attacks? "I thought: Uh-oh. We're at war," said Rose Matsushita of Bellevue, Washington. "Some of them [people of Arab background] are here. And they were probably going to go through the same thing we did."[8]

The outcry for internment of the West Coast Japanese came swiftly after the Pearl Harbor bombing. After

For many people, the terrorist attacks on September 11, 2001, brought back memories of the shock and horror of Pearl Harbor.

September 11, in contrast, President George W. Bush asked the public not to blame innocent Arab Americans for what had happened. Few people demanded that all Arab Americans be held behind barbed wire. Nevertheless, Arab Americans and aliens from Muslim nations were under suspicion. Thousands were arrested and imprisoned without charges. Racial profiling was a key factor in these arrests. In racial profiling, a person is considered to be a crime suspect largely on the basis of his or her racial or ethnic background.

"Before September 11 we had almost succeeded in eliminating racial profiling," stated Michel Shehadeh of the American-Arab Anti-Discrimination Committee. "After September 11 it's a whole new world. One thousand Arab Americans have already been detained [in December, 2001] and we don't know who they are and what charges have been brought against them."[9]

Officials said that the arrest and questioning of Arabs and other Muslims was necessary for national security. Many Americans found this argument deeply troubling. Of course the nation should work to prevent terrorist attacks. At the same time, however, the constitutional rights of Americans must be respected and preserved. Kabzuag Vaj of the Asian Freedom Project in Madison, Wisconsin, expressed his concern in an interview. "Talking to the mainstream about racial profiling is hard," he said. "The excuse people give us is [that] extreme times demand extreme measures, whatever is necessary to catch the terrorists."[10]

Lawyers from the American Civil Liberties Union (ACLU) work to protect the civil rights of US citizens. The ACLU defended a number of Arab Americans whose rights seemed to have been violated. An ACLU spokesperson wrote: "We bring these lawsuits because, as a nation, we long ago settled the issue of discrimination. We declared it to be wrong, immoral, and contrary to fundamental American values. We also made it illegal."[11]

Survivors of the Japanese-American internment watched the rise of racial profiling with dismay. "There are things [occurring] that are really disturbing today that in some ways echo what had happened to us," said John Tateishi, director of the JACL. "I felt that it was our responsibility to speak out and take a very strong position."[12]

With the wisdom of hindsight, most Americans today see the World War II internment of Japanese Americans as a grievous mistake. Some people, however, still try to downplay what happened. W.W. Hastings, a World War II veteran from Bishop, California, stated:

> The Japanese were free to come and go [from Manzanar.]—all it was was an assembly center. They were escorted there not to keep them under control, but just to protect them. It did have a loose barbed-wire fence, but I saw them sneaking out all the time to go fishing.[13]

A few voices still claim that Roosevelt's decision was fully justified. In 2004, a conservative Asian-American newspaper columnist named Michelle Malkin published a book called *In Defense of Internment: The Case for Racial Profiling in World War II and the War on Terror.* Malkin argued that an active spy network existed among the West Coast Japanese. She claimed that the internment was necessary and suggested that similar measures might be needed to control Arab terrorism. Malkin was not the first to put forth these ideas. Over the years, a handful of historians and writers have insisted that the Japanese Americans were indeed a military threat. A few contend that the facts about the internment have been grossly exaggerated. Now and then, someone states that the internment never really happened at all. "They come out of the woodwork," says Hiro Fugii. "I don't understand how they can say those things. They just don't know."[14]

A Japanese American holds up a photograph of herself (sitting on the steps) and her family at the Topaz, Utah, internment camp during a church's Day of Remembrance to honor those who were detained during World War II.

In the years after 9/11, volunteers worked to establish the ten World War II internment camps as state or national historic landmarks. Many of the volunteers were former internees and their children and grandchildren. Each camp set up its own committee or foundation. Volunteers contacted funders and legislators, arguing for the site's preservation. The groups rescued tracts of land from developers. They restored barracks and recreation halls and planned fascinating interactive displays.

A woman comforts her mother, a former detainee, at a memorial for the inhabitants of the Rohwer, Arkansas, internment camp.

Little by little, they raised the camps from the deserts and swamps where they lay buried. Thanks to the hard work of many, today these camps are all historic landmarks and reminders of the injustices suffered by so many innocent people.

In the spring of 2013, the Japanese American Internment Museum in McGehee, Arkansas, opened its doors to the public. This area in southeast Arkansas was the site of two internment camps: Rohwer just to the north and Jerome to the south. The camps, the only two in the eastern half of the United States, were the temporary homes of seventeen thousand Japanese Americans. The museum displays artifacts, photographs, recordings, and artwork collected from former internees and their families.

Actor George Takei was interned at Rohwer along with his family and spoke at the museum's opening. He described his parents' frustration and anger at being detained and stressed the importance of appreciating the rights that come along with citizenship. "We must know what it means to be an American citizen and how precious our rights are," he declared.[15] Like other museums located on the sites of internment camps, this exhibit is a way to educate current and future generations about a dark time in American history. In doing so, these monuments may help to ensure that the mistakes of the past are not repeated.

TIMELINE

1849 Chinese immigrants come to California to look for gold; many establish businesses that serve miners from the eastern United States.

1867 The first Japanese immigrants come to study and work in the United States.

1882 The United States passes the Chinese Exclusion Law, putting an end to immigration from China.

1884 The Japanese government allows landless laborers to emigrate to Hawaii.

1900 Japanese immigration increases steadily, though the numbers remain small compared to other groups.

1907 President Theodore Roosevelt makes the Gentlemen's Agreement in which Japanese children will attend school with white pupils in San Francisco, and Japan will end the immigration of Japanese laborers to the United States.

1913 California is the first state to pass an "alien land law," making it impossible for persons born in Japan to buy land.

1924 President Calvin Coolidge signs the Asian Exclusion Act, putting an end to all immigration from Asian countries.

1931 Under an aggressive military government, Japan invades Manchuria.

1941 December 7: Japanese planes bomb the US naval base at Pearl Harbor in Hawaii.

1942 February 19: President Franklin D. Roosevelt issues Executive Order 9066, calling for the relocation of "any and all persons" away from designated military zones on the West Coast.

May: The army moves some one hundred ten thousand Japanese Americans from the West Coast into assembly centers.

Fall: Ten relocation camps are opened to house the evacuees.

December 6: A riot ensues at Manzanar Relocation Camp after internees beat a man suspected of spying for the camp administration.

1943—February	The War Relocation Authority (WRA) orders internees to complete a form expressing their loyalty to the United States; large numbers of students and laborers are allowed to leave the camps and settle in the East and Midwest.
1943	An all-Nisei regiment, the 442nd, is formed to fight on the European front.
1945—January	The WRA announces plans to close the camps. **August 6:** US planes drop an atomic bomb on Hiroshima, Japan.
1946—Spring	The last internees leave the camps. **June 30:** The WRA ceases operations.
1952	The McCarran-Walter Act allows persons born in Asia to become naturalized citizens of the United States.
1964	The last federal compensation cases for former internees are settled.
1973	Some fifteen hundred camp survivors and their families make the first annual pilgrimage to Manzanar Relocation Center.
1988	The Civil Liberties Act of 1988 calls for each survivor of the internment camps to receive a redress from the federal government in the amount of $20,000.
1992	The Civil Liberties Act Amendments of 1992 allocate an additional $400 million to ensure that all survivors receive their redress.
2001	Congress declares ten detention sites will be preserved as historical landmarks.
2010	President Obama awards the Congressional Gold Medal to members of the 100th Battalion, the 442nd Regimental Combat Team for heroism in World War II.
2011	California celebrates its first Fred Korematsu Day, in honor of the Japanese American who fought the internment order and became a civil rights activist.
2013	The Japanese American Internment Museum opens in McGehee, Arkansas.

CHAPTER NOTES

Chapter 1. The Journey Begins

1. Jean Wakatsuke Houston and James B. Houston, *Farewell to Manzanar* (New York: Ember, 2012), 8.
2. "Why Was Pearl Harbor Attacked?" *Pearl Harbor Oahu*, 2013, https://www.pearlharboroahu.com/attack.htm.
3. Mary Matsuda Gruenwald, *Looking Like the Enemy: My Story of Imprisonment in Japanese-American Internment Camps* (Troutdale, Oreg.: NewSage Publishing, 2005), 24.
4. Ibid., 25.
5. Ibid.
6. Gary Y. Okihioro, ed., *Encyclopedia of Japanese American Internment* (Santa Barbara, Calif.: ABC-CLIO, 2012), 42.

Chapter 2. Settling in America

1. Hamilton Holt, ed., *The Life Stories of Undistinguished Americans, as Told by Themselves, Expanded Edition* (New York: Routledge, 2001), 161.
2. Ibid., 166.
3. Sandra C. Taylor, *Jewel of the Desert: Japanese American Internment at Topaz* (Berkeley, Calif.: University of California Press, 1993), 8–9.
4. US Census Bureau, "Region and Country or Area of Birth of the Foreign-Born Population…1900: Japan," last modified October 31, 2011, http://www.census.gov/population/www/documentation/twps0029/tab04.html.
5. David A. Neiwert, *Strawberry Days: How Internment Destroyed a Japanese American Community* (New York: Palgrave/Macmillan, 2005), 40.
6. Ibid., 12.
7. Quoted in Ibid., 12–13.
8. Ibid., 17.
9. Ibid., 18.
10. Taylor, 11.
11. Ibid., 10.
12. Neiwert, 56.

13. Greg Robinson, *By Order of the President: FDR and the Internment of Japanese Americans* (Cambridge, Mass.: Harvard University Press, 2001), 30–31.

14. Sue Kunitomi Embrey, "From Manzanar to the Present: A Personal Journey," in *Last Witnesses: Reflections on the Wartime Internment of Japanese Americans,* ed. Erica Harth (New York: Palgrave/St. Martin's Press, 2001), 168.

15. Gordon H. Chang, ed., *Morning Glory, Evening Shadow: Yamato Ichihashi and His Internment Writings, 1942–1945* (Stanford, Calif.: Stanford University Press, 1997), 58.

Chapter 3. State of Fear

1. Arthur A. Hansen, ed., *Japanese American World War II Evacuation Oral History Project, Part I: Internees* (Westport, Conn.: Meckler Publishing, 1991), 56.

2. Ibid., 56–57.

3. Ibid., 59, 82.

4. Harry H. L. Kitano, *Japanese Americans: The Evolution of a Subculture* (Englewood Cliffs, N.J.: Prentice-Hall, 1976), 70.

5. Peter Irons. *Justice at War* (Berkeley, Calif.: University of California Press, 1983), 19.

6. David A. Neiwert, *Strawberry Days: How Internment Destroyed a Japanese American Community* (New York: Palgrave/Macmillan, 2005), 149–150.

7. Ibid., 108.

8. Lawson Fusao Inada, ed., *Only What We Could Carry: The Japanese American Internment Experience* (Berkeley, Calif.: Heyday Books, 2000), 16.

9. Kitano, 71.

10. Erica Harth, ed., *Last Witnesses: Reflections on the Wartime Internment of Japanese Americans* (New York: Palgrave/St. Martin's Press, 2001), 12.

11. Neiwert, 121.

12. Jacobus tenBroek, Edward N. Barnhart, and Floyd Matson, *Prejudice, War and the Constitution* (Berkeley, Calif.: University of California, 1968), 263.

13. Greg Robinson, *By Order of the President: FDR and the Internment of Japanese Americans* (Cambridge, Mass.: Harvard University Press, 2001), 11.

14. Ibid., 67.

15. Ibid., 120.

16. Ibid., 252.
17. Michi Weglyn, *Years of Infamy: The Untold Story of America's Concentration Camps* (New York: William Morrow, 1976), 69.
18. Robinson, 112.
19. Neiwert, 138.
20. Kitano, 78.
21. Ibid., 79.
22. Robinson, 155.
23. Sandra C. Taylor, *Jewel of the Desert: Japanese American Internment at Topaz* (Berkeley, Calif.: University of California Press, 1993), 52.
24. Neiwert, 135.
25. Ibid., 139–140.

Chapter 4. Camp Life

1. Martin W. Sandler, *Imprisoned: The Betrayal of Japanese Americans During World War II* (New York: Bloomsbury, 2013), 57.
2. Mary Matsuda Gruenwald, *Looking Like the Enemy: My Story of Imprisonment in Japanese-American Internment Camps* (Troutdale, Oreg.: NewSage Publishing, 2005), 47.
3. Hiro Fugii, interview with the author, Oakland, Calif., December 9, 2005.
4. Ibid.
5. Michi Weglyn, *Years of Infamy: The Untold Story of America's Concentration Camps* (New York: William Morrow, 1976), 81.
6. Ibid., 82.
7. Jean Wakatsuke Houston and James B. Houston, *Farewell to Manzanar* (New York: Ember, 2012), 31–32.
8. Gruenwald, 57.
9. Gordon H. Chang, ed., *Morning Glory, Evening Shadow: Yamato Ichihashi and His Internment Writings, 1942–1945* (Stanford, Calif.: Stanford University Press, 1997), 133.
10. Sandra C. Taylor, *Jewel of the Desert: Japanese American Internment at Topaz* (Berkeley, Calif.: University of California Press, 1993), 91.
11. Chang, 122.
12. Gruenwald, 87.
13. Taylor, 93–94.
14. Weglyn, 21.
15. John Tateishi, "Memories From Behind Barbed Wire," in *Last Witnesses: Reflections on the Wartime Internment of Japanese*

Americans, ed. Erica Harth (New York: Palgrave/St. Martin's Press, 2001), 132.

16. Harry H. L. Kitano, *Japanese Americans: The Evolution of a Subculture* (Englewood Cliffs, N.J.: Prentice-Hall, 1976), 73–74.

17. Tateishi, 132.

18. "Tule Lake Internment Camp Exhibit," J. Willard Marriott Library, accessed March 30, 2015, http://www.lib.utah.edu/collections/photo-exhibits/tule-lake.php.

19. George E. Brown, "Return to Gila River," in *Last Witnesses: Reflections on the Wartime Internment of Japanese Americans*, ed. Erica Harth (New York: Palgrave/St. Martin's Press, 2001), 123.

20. Greg Robinson, *By Order of the President: FDR and the Internment of Japanese Americans* (Cambridge, Mass.: Harvard University Press, 2001), 112.

21. Arthur A. Hansen, ed., *Japanese American World War II Evacuation Oral History Project, Part I: The Internees* (Westport, Conn.: Meckler Publishing, 1991), 206.

22. Chang, 206–207.

23. Milton Meltzer, *Dorothea Lange: A Photographer's Life* (New York: Farrar Straus Giroux, 1978), 243.

24. Erica Harth, "Democracy for Beginners," in *Last Witnesses: Reflections on the Wartime Internment of Japanese Americans*, ed. Erica Harth (New York: Palgrave/Macmillan, 2001), 197.

Chapter 5. A Way Out

1. Hiro Fugii, interview with the author, Oakland, Calif., December 9, 2005.

2. Arthur A. Hansen, *Japanese American World War II Evacuation Oral History Project, Part I: Internees* (Westport, Conn.: Meckler Publishing, 1991), 112.

3. Ibid., 255.

4. Jean Wakatsuke Houston and James B. Houston, *Farewell to Manzanar* (New York: Ember, 2012), 74.

5. Greg Robinson, *By Order of the President: FDR and the Internment of Japanese Americans* (Cambridge, Mass.: Harvard University Press, 2001), 200.

6. Mary Matsuda Gruenwald, *Looking Like the Enemy: My Story of Imprisonment in Japanese-American Internment Camps* (Troutdale, Oreg.: NewSage Publishing, 2005), 131.

7. Gary Y. Okihiro, ed., *Encyclopedia of Japanese Internment* (Santa Barbara, Calif.: ABC-CLIO, 2012), 102.

8. Houston and Houston, 84.

9. Gruenwald, 249.

10. Roger Daniels, *Concentration Camps, USA: Japanese Americans and World War II* (New York: Holt, Rinehart and Winston, 1972), 115.

11. Ibid., 100.

12. Gary Y. Okihioro, ed., *Encyclopedia of Japanese American Internment* (Santa Barbara, Calif.: ABC-CLIO, 2012), 63–64.

13. Michi Weglyn, *Years of Infamy: The Untold Story of America's Concentration Camps* (New York: William Morrow, 1976), 98–99.

14. Ibid., 100.

Chapter 6. The Opening of the Gates

1. Roger Daniels, *Concentration Camps, USA: Japanese Americans and World War II* (New York: Holt, Rinehart and Winston, 1972), 153.

2. Ibid.

3. Sandra C. Taylor, *Jewel of the Desert: Japanese American Internment at Topaz* (Berkeley, Calif.: University of California Press, 1993), 218.

4. Michi Weglyn, *Years of Infamy: The Untold Story of America's Concentration Camps* (New York: William Morrow, 1976), 246.

5. Daniels, 166.

6. Gordon H. Chang, ed., *Morning Glory, Evening Shadow: Yamato Ichihashi and His Internment Writings, 1942–1945* (Stanford, Calif.: Stanford University Press, 1997), 373.

7. Daniels, 167.

8. Weglyn, 251.

9. David A. Neiwert, *Strawberry Days: How Internment Destroyed a Japanese American Community* (New York: Palgrave/Macmillan, 2005), 198.

10. Daniels, 165.

11. Neiwert, 209.

12. Weglyn, 268.

13. Taylor, 276.

14. Neiwert, 221.

15. Taylor, 212–213.

16. Neiwert, 193.

17. Harry H. L. Kitano, *Japanese Americans: The Evolution of a Subculture* (Englewood Cliffs, N.J.: Prentice-Hall, 1976), 89.

18. Arthur A. Hansen, ed., *Japanese American World War II Evacuation Oral History Project, Part I: Internees* (Westport, Conn.: Meckler Publishing, 1991), 205.

Chapter 7. Rebuilding Dreams

1. Martin W. Sandler, *Imprisoned: The Betrayal of Japanese Americans During World War II* (New York: Bloomsbury, 2013), 166.
2. Mary Matsuda Gruenwald, *Looking Like the Enemy: My Story of Imprisonment in Japanese-American Internment Camps* (Troutdale, Oreg.: NewSage Publishing, 2005), 205.
3. Mitsuye Yamada, "Legacy of Silence (I)," in *Last Witnesses: Reflections on the Wartime Internment of Japanese Americans*, ed. Erica Harth (New York: Palgrave/St. Martin's Press, 2001), 35.
4. David A. Neiwert, *Strawberry Days: How Internment Destroyed a Japanese American Community* (New York: Palgrave/Macmillan, 2005), 244.
5. Sue Kunitomi Embrey, "From Manzanar to the Present: A Personal Journey," in *Last Witnesses: Reflections on the Wartime Internment of Japanese Americans*, ed. Erica "Harth (New York: Palgrave/Macmillan, 2001), 179.
6. Greg Robinson, *By Order of the President: FDR and the Internment of Japanese Americans* (Cambridge, Mass.: Harvard University Press, 2001), 251.
7. Neiwert, 236–237.
8. Ibid., 235.
9. "The Slippery Slope," *Alternet*, December 13, 2001, http://www.alternet.org/story/12079.
10. Ibid.
11. "ACLU Sues Four Major Airlines Over Discrimination Against Passengers," *American Civil Liberties Union*, June 4, 2002, http//:www.aclu.org/racialjustice/racialprofiling/15867prs20020604.html.
12. Neiwert, 237.
13. Erica Harth, ed., *Last Witnesses* (New York: Palgrave/ St. Martin's Press, 2001), 11.
14. Hiro Fugii, interview with the author, Oakland, Calif., December 9, 2005.
15. "Japanese American Internment Museum, Exhibits Dedicated at McGehee," *Arkansas State University*, April 16, 2013, http://www.astate.edu/a/asunews/newsDetails.dot?newsid=0d8f43ab-9c5a-4785-9508-515f6ae3ce60.

GLOSSARY

alien—Person born in a foreign country and/or holding foreign citizenship.

assimilate—To blend in, become part of.

Caucasian—Belonging to the white, or European, race.

compensation—Repayment.

discrimination—Behavior that treats members of one group differently from members of another.

duress—Force used to change a person's opinion or influence his or her choice.

executive order—An order given by the president.

internment—Imprisonment.

Issei—A first-generation immigrant from Japan.

naturalized citizen—A person who becomes a citizen by living in a country for a given length of time and meeting certain other requirements.

Nisei—A second-generation Japanese American, born in the United States of Japanese-born parents.

pact—A solemn agreement.

picture bride—A Japanese woman who married her husband sight unseen, based on an exchange of photographs.

racial profiling—Suspicion of a person or persons based on race or ethnic background.

redress—Payment made as a form of apology for wrongdoing.

relocation center—A place to which a group of people are moved in a crisis or emergency.

sabotage—An act that intentionally damages a factory, military base, or other facility.

Sansei—A third-generation Japanese immigrant to the United States, grandchildren of the Issei.

segregation—The separation of one group from another, based on a characteristic, such as race, gender, or disability.

Shikata ga nai—Japanese phrase meaning, "It can't be helped."

vandals—People who destroy property out of malice.

FURTHER READING

Books

Hay, Jeff, ed. *The Internment of Japanese Americans.* Farmington Hills, Mich.: Greenhaven Press, 2012.

Houston, Jeanne Wakatsuki, and James D. Houston. *Farewell to Manzanar.* New York: Ember, 2012.

Kenney, Karen Latchana. *Korematsu v. The United States: World War II Japanese-American Internment Camps.* Edina, Minn.: Abdo, 2012.

Sandler, Martin W. *Imprisoned: The Betrayal of Japanese Americans During World War II.* New York: Bloomsbury, 2013.

Wukovitz, John. *Internment of Japanese Americans.* San Diego: Lucent, 2012.

Web Sites

asianamericanmedia.org/jainternment
Learn about Japanese-American internment through video clips, text, and photos.

janm.org/collections
View an online collection of letters, art, photos, and other artifacts from the internment camps.

calisphere.universityofcalifornia.edu/jarda/
Primary sources, oral histories, and interactive displays provide insight into Japanese-American internment.

INDEX